Requiem

Of A

Champion: Two

Seconds from Glory

A Racer's Reflections and
Remembrances

Mitch Grant

A recently retired, championship-winning, road racing driver's reflections, and remembrances, about his long career competing on America's top racing circuits. This book explores the origins of his lifelong love for the sport- a passion kindled as a child by the glamour of the nearby Sebring Twelve Hours of Endurance. It describes his struggles as a young man to compete in the sport he loved so much. And, in detail, reviews the successes, failures, lessons, and regrets from nearly thirty years of racing (both at amateur, and professional, levels).

The book describes many of the key American racing circuits upon which the author competed during his career. As part of this description he discusses his thoughts on some of the right, and wrong, ways to negotiate the most important corners on these tracks. The author also takes the time to describe the occasional crashes and wrecks that marred his, otherwise, successful racing career. As part of those descriptions he analyzes the causes of those misadventures, and, where appropriate, assigns blame to the guilty parties.

He also shares with the reader his most important **"Speed Secrets"**- twelve lessons learned from his decades of competing against some of the most (and least) talented road racers in America.

The author uses this book to reflect on what racing has meant to him, and why. And, to document, and to thank, the many people whose assistance helped him to achieve what he was able to accomplish in racing. This book will, hopefully, appeal to anyone who truly loves sports car racing- at any level. It is a racing remembrance written by a man whose love for the sport is deep; and for those who share that same passion.

Dedication

This book is dedicated to SCCA Corner Workers everywhere- volunteers who give of themselves tirelessly to ensure safe and successful road racing- purely because of their own love for the sport. Thank you.

Any net royalties from the sale of this book will be donated to the SCCA Central Florida Region's Workers Fund.

Introitus

"Automobile Racing: The most fun you can have with your clothes on!"

I have sometimes questioned whether the qualifier in this often quoted line- which essentially ranks the joy of sex above the thrills of competitive driving- is accurate. Now- don't get me wrong- I very much enjoy making love to my wife. Always have, and always will. But, I loved automobile racing, too.

Readers may note that I discussed love making in the present (and, hopefully, future) tense; but, I mentioned auto racing using only the past tense. I did that intentionally, since I have recently retired, after almost thirty years of competition, from driving racing cars. This book is being written because of that decision.

Why write a book about something you have decided to no longer do? Why write a book about something that, at its heart, is a personal, and intensely selfish, activity- an experience that can never be truly shared? I've not decided to do this to try to somehow offer a justification for what, at the end of the day, has in essence always been a foolish activity. I've not decided to do this because I expect to sell many of these books. After all, who other than a few dear friends who participated with me in this foolishness, would ever want to read this? And, I hope, this book will not come across as an attempt to apologize to those who may have suffered while I was having so much fun. I recognize fully the dishonesty that such an attempt would represent.

Rather, I'm doing this to explain what racing has meant to me. And, to document some of these activities before they all disappear forever into the mist of nothingness. And, most importantly, I'm writing this book to honor, and show my love for, this sport and for those who participated in it with me.

I have titled the book as a "Requiem." By way of explanation, the dictionary says that this term comes from the opening words of the Catholic Mass for the Dead: *"Requiem aeternam dona eis, Domine: et lux perpetua luceat eis."* The internet has translated this for me as follows: *"Grant them eternal rest, Lord; and may perpetual light shine on them."* Commonly a requiem is a religious ceremony performed for the dead. But, in a nonreligious context the word refers simply to an act of remembrance. I am, of course, not yet dead. Neither am I, in any conventional sense, a religious person. I hope, however, that since what I want to do is to honor, show love for, and remember, a sport that has meant so much to me- the use of this term is appropriate.

Mitch Grant

March 27, 2017

Sanctus: … "Heaven and Earth Are Full of Your Glory. Hosanna in the Highest!"

James M. "Jimmy" Grant

Myrtle L. Bridges Grant

Sherry A. Hardin Grant

Jamie Danielle Johnson

Kathryn Elizabeth Shores

Mike Scharnow

Mark Scharnow

Chris Scharnow

Bill Wilkins

John Schunzel

John Pettit

Cass Whitehead

Brad Creger

Dan Hiner

Lance Stewart

Mitch Payton

Fran Broadfoot

Hector DeLa Torriente, Sr.

Dennis Sprague

Carolyn Sprague

Rodney Thompson

Terry Earwood

SCCA Workers

Phil Hill

Jimmy Clark

Dan Gurney

Pedro Rodriquez

John Surtees

Peter Gregg

Mark Donohue

Mario Andretti

Fred Lewis

Mick Robinson

Dan Nye

Book One: The *Kyrie Eleison*

Lord, Have Mercy on Us.

Christ, Have Mercy on Us.

Lord, Have Mercy on Us.

Chapter One: The End!

I started my final race on pole; and finished it more than two laps ahead of the closest competitor- a result that wrapped up my third consecutive endurance driving championship. I remember thinking as I went under that waving checkered flag- "there can never be a better time to quit racing than now!" Even then I couldn't come to grips with making a conscious decision to retire - but, I definitely knew that the time to address that issue was nearing.

That last race was a seventy five minute endurance event held on the Homestead Motor Speedway, one of my favorite tracks. The course configuration used was the "Modified Road Course," a layout that combines an infield road course with nearly 80% of the speedway. The track's long back straight leads directly into NASCAR's high- banked turns 3 and 4, before flowing onto the track's front straight. Together this stretch of mirror smooth track makes up one of the longest, and consequently fastest, bits that we race on anywhere. The car that I drove that day, a SCCA Spec Racer Ford Gen 3, could achieve one hundred and fifty miles per hour- almost fast enough for an amateur racer like me. At the end of the front straight, at the point where your speed is the highest, the track bends left off of the speedway and into the first turn of the infield. This turn is taken flat out in cars like the one I was driving. Flat out means your right foot is still holding the accelerator all the way to the floor- the same position it's been in (other than when shifting to a higher gear) since you entered the back straight- a little over a mile before. Going through a corner at one hundred and fifty miles per hour is one of the greatest thrills you can have in racing. And, it's one of the reasons that I loved this track.

As soon as you pass the apex of this corner you have to contend with a massive bump as the car transitions from the banked front straight onto the flat infield. You feel the car bottom out, and have to wait for it to rebound and settle from that bounce, and only then do you dare to take your foot off the accelerator, and forcefully apply the brakes to slow for the rapidly approaching second turn- a ninety degree bend to the left. At this point you begin threshold braking for the corner (a term that means you are on the threshold of lock up- using all of the capacity of the brakes and tires to slow the car). At the instant that you first apply the brakes the resulting force of deceleration instantly transfers weight to the front of the car. This increased load on the front tires means that you can brake even more aggressively. But, once the force of deceleration ebbs, and as that transferred load begins to return to its static position, you must gradually, steadily, relieve pressure on the brake pedal in order to prevent the front tires from locking up and sliding. It is critical to remember that the amount of traction available is always a function of the mechanical grip between the tire and the road, multiplied times the amount of weight acting to force the tire into the surface. This same concept applies, not only to braking, but also to accelerating, cornering, and to any combination of the above.

Your desired result in this braking exercise, beyond merely slowing the car, is to position the vehicle, in the least possible time, at that exact inch of track where it needs to be in order to turn in to achieve the perfect arc through the next corner- at the exact maximum speed at which the car will be able to make that upcoming theoretical arc. If you are moving too fast when you attempt to turn, the car won't be able to steer and instead it will simply slide wide causing you to either leave the track, or to have to slow even more to be able to finally make the corner. But, if you've slowed too much before turning, then you will have simply lost valuable time. And, even if your speed is absolutely correct, if you turn in too early, then you will need to slow to finally make your way around the following corner. But, if you turn in too late, you will not be able to use the maximum radius line through the corner- causing you to have to go around it more slowly. Of course, making any of these mistakes will mean that you will have lost valuable time in negotiating the turn.

But, brake pedal pressure, weight transfer, steering, speed, tire slip, and turn in points are not the only things you have to consider as you attempt to get around the next corner. At the same time you also will need to manipulate the car's transmission to ensure that it will be in the proper gear to enable the driver to accelerate, at maximum speed, out of the following corner. To do this at Homestead's first set of turns requires that the driver shift from fifth gear, the ratio in which the car entered the turn, into fourth, and then into third gear, the ratio that will be required to accelerate at full force through the following corner. Unfortunately, to do this properly in an older-style racing ca, equipped with a manual transmission, is far more complicated than simply moving the shift lever from one position to another. It's critical to do this in a way that the balance of the car is not upset, even to the slightest degree, as you brake, and prepare to corner. One of the very easiest ways to spin a car is to let out the clutch when the speeds of the engine and transmission are not properly matched. If you do this you will cause a shock transfer of weight from the rear wheels onto the front. And, should that happen the now lightly loaded rear tires will instantly lose all traction, and the car will spin instantly around the newly highly loaded front tires. Yes- smooth footwork as you brake, and shift, is critical!

The best way accomplish the dual tasks of braking and downshifting is to use what is known as the "heel and toe" technique- a process that allows the driver to simultaneously manipulate the brake and accelerator pedals. To do this you place the upper left side of the driver's right foot and toes on the brake pedal. Then, as you begin to brake, the driver depresses the clutch with his left foot, and moves the gear lever out of fifth gear (the slowing of engine speed and resulting reduction in torque will allow the lever to easily disengage itself). While still applying, and without disrupting, the maximum desired braking force with the left side of your right foot, you roll your right ankle and leg in such a way that the right edge of the foot depresses the accelerator. As you do this you also release the clutch while simultaneously revving the engine to produce a transmission speed that will allow it to smoothly accept the next selected gear. Then, you declutch again, move the lever into the next gear, and release the clutch. And, that's just to get you from fifth to fourth gear. The process needs to be repeated to get into the ultimately desired third gear. And, all of this has to take place as you're desperately trying to slow the car, balancing it on the absolute edge of control, while trying to position the car at the proper point, and proper speed, to make the next corner!

How long do you have to do this? Only seconds! Not nearly enough time to be able to even think about everything you're doing as you're actually doing it. And, never enough time to look steadily at your intended destination, the turn-in point for the following corner. Instead, you can only give that approaching target a fleeting glance. Eyes are the most important asset for a racing driver, and given the speed at which you are travelling, they must always be looking up and ahead- focused not on your immediate target, but looking instead at the point you need to go to next.

Time! In racing everything eventually comes down to time. The objective for the driver is to minimize how long it takes to drive around the track. Most teams utilize a variety of techniques to help their drivers try to achieve that goal. Every lap is, of course, clocked. Frequently, the driver's time through various segments of the course will also be tracked. Most teams will also measure the time it takes their drivers to negotiate each individual turn. And, beyond that, some will also clock the time it takes the driver to go through specific segments of each turn. Time means everything. Given this fixation on time, good drivers are usually referred to not, as you might expect, as being fast, but rather, as being "quick." Slower drivers search desperately for how to save seconds on the track; average drivers look for tenths of a second; and great drivers stress over gaining or losing hundredths of a second. There is a reason that the sport's very best drivers- those in Formula 1- earn so much money. Most people can't even comprehend differences this small.

I've shared the detail of what is required to successfully maneuver a racing car quickly around one small portion of one track to demonstrate just how challenging driving a racing car can be. And to set the stage for understanding just how rewarding it can be when it all is done correctly. Multiply those challenges by the hundreds of other similar actions and decisions required to successfully, and quickly, negotiate just one lap of a track, and it's easy to see why driving a racing car quickly is so difficult- and so very, very addictive! And, why I loved doing it so much.

Chapter Two: The Beginning

I've wondered often about when, and why, automobile racing became so important to me. Was it nature? Was it nurture? Truthfully, even today, I'm not sure of the answer. But, I do know that some of my earliest childhood memories involved, in one way or another, vehicles. For example, I remember adamantly telling my parents as a very young child that my life's ambition was to grow up to be a fertilizer truck driver! I seem to recall that, while they thought that was cute, they may have other career plans in mind for me.

My earliest years were spent in Pierce, Florida. This community was actually a company town- owned by the American Agricultural Fertilizer Company. All the town's houses, including ours, were owned by the company. There was a town commissary; a town switchboard; and a town utility system. Everything in town was, in fact, owned by the company. Our house was located on a corner lot on one of the town's busiest intersections- semi-trucks and trailers hauling fertilizer came by nearly constantly. Across the street was the company's railroad track. Long trains of gondola cars loaded with freshly mined phosphate rock came into town to dump at the company's storage and processing facility.

I remember always being intrigued with those trains. I'd often sit in the yard and wave at the engineers and conductors as they passed. But, I was warned by my parents to never go across the street to the tracks. They explained that doing this could be very dangerous. And, being a good kid I, of course, obeyed. Obeyed, that is, up until when I got a wagon for my birthday- I don't remember for sure, but I'm guessing that it was for my fourth birthday.

And, like most four year old kids, I was now beginning to reason things out. And, of course, I had a new wagon. And, what good is a new wagon if it's empty? Wagons, like semi trucks and trailers, are, of course, meant for hauling stuff. And, the largest supply of haulable stuff that I could find were the rocks that secured the ties and rails of the tracks across the street. Of course, I knew that I wasn't supposed to go onto those tracks, but I reasoned that Mom would surely understand that securing a wagon load of rocks to haul was an important enough reason for me to disobey, just once, their important rule. And, being an observant kid, I was pretty certain that I'd figured out how frequently the trains came, and that I would have plenty of time to load the wagon and come back into the yard before the next train would return. So, I confidently drug my wagon across the street, down the embankment to the track, and carefully positioned my wagon over one of the rails where I'd have access to all of the very best stones. Then I happily proceeded to load my wagon full of granite. I remember stepping back to admire the load that was now spilling over the sides of the Radio Flyer. I was going to have all of the rocks that I could every want. All I had to do now was pull the wagon off the tracks, up the embankment, across the street, into the yard, and all would be good. So I proudly and happily grabbed the handle on the tongue of the wagon to begin my homeward journey. But, then I discovered the one flaw in my grand plan. The loaded wagon was heavy. So heavy, in fact, that my wagon was stuck! I pulled, and I pulled. But, I couldn't yank it over the iron rail that it straddled. And, then…..and, then….. and, then…. the train started coming!

I actually don't remember many of the details immediately after that. But, I do know that the engineer was able to stop the train before it crushed my wagon. I seem to remember that he may have then blown the train's whistle long enough that Mom came out of the house to see what was going on. And, I remember that Dad arrived shortly after. And, I definitely remember that when he arrived he was mad! He embarrassedly apologized to the engineer that his kid had stopped the company's train. Then he dumped the rocks out of my wagon, and removed it from the track. Then, in the house, he explained, with the assistance of his belt, the consequences of disobeying his rules. I know that I never went onto that train track again, and I'm pretty sure that I lost the use of my wagon for a long time. Yes, it's safe to conclude that, even at a very young age, trucks, trains, and other things with wheels had made a big impression on me.

Shortly after that incident the company made the decision to dissolve its town. Consequently, all residents were told that they would have to leave. But, if you wanted, you could have your house- that is, if you would agree to move it out of town. The company even provided nearby lots that residents could move their houses to. My parents agreed to take "their" house. But, for some reason, made the decision to forego the company-provided lot, and instead, bought one "in town." Town, in this case, was the nearby community of Mulberry, Florida. I think that the proximity of the purchased lot to the newly constructed high school was the deciding factor. Far better, I suspect, for my sister and I to eventually walk to school than for someone to have to drive us. And, that's how I came to grow up in the "Phosphate Mining Capital of the World."

So what does any of this have to do with my love for racing? Maybe, nothing. But, in a small mining town, other than high school football, there wasn't much that was exciting, colorful, and interesting. Perhaps that's why I can still vividly remember, while my mother was buying the family's food, sitting on the dusty floor of the town's largest grocery store, at the foot of the periodical rack, perusing available automobile magazines. I was probably ten years old. It was then that I discovered sports cars, and more importantly, sports car racing. For some unexplained reason I found myself totally mesmerized by the articles, and pictures, I discovered in *Sports Car Graphic*, and *Road &Track*. I could have cared less about *Hot Rod*, or *Motor Trend*, or the others that focused on domestic automobiles. Neither, was I interested in the hunting, fishing, football, baseball, or golfing periodicals- none of these did much for me. But, I was absolutely fascinated by the images of Ferraris, Maseratis, and other exotic automobiles roaring around the race tracks of Europe, driven by handsome, daring, and glamorous young men seemingly oblivious to the dangers of what they were doing. And, what was almost unbelievable was that some of the best of these heroes were actually Americans. Phil Hill, for example, was driving for Ferrari! Dan Gurney, a crew-cut wearing kid from California, was driving for Porsche. Handsome Carroll Shelby, a chicken farmer from Texas, was another American standout. And, a young, goofy-looking guy who wore even thicker eye glasses than me- Masten Gregory- was there, too. And, despite his vision shortcomings, he was quick- and, fearless. Damn! If he could make it, I could, too.

For me, reading about this stuff sure beat watching dirty pick-up trucks and clumsy station wagons lazily motoring through the pot-holed punctured streets of my tiny boring town. Shortly after, I remember telling Mom that what I wanted for Christmas more than anything else was a subscription to *Sports Car Graphic*!

Chapter Three: Sebring!

Without question, the car magazines were the bait on the hook-bait that I swallowed enthusiastically, happily, and passionately. But, what really set the hook- set it so deeply that I have never been able to get it out- was attending the 1963 Sebring 12 Hour Gran Prix of Endurance.

Sebring, Florida, at least by my pre-teen standards, was a mid-sized Florida city. After all, it had a population back then almost 5 times greater than the number of residents that lived in my town. It was located only sixty miles to the southeast of Mulberry. You could drive to it, if you had any reason to go there, in a little over an hour. But, I had never been to Sebring, and likely I might never have visited, if it hadn't been for one important fact. That fact, amazingly, was that one of the world's most important, and most prestigious, sports car races was held annually in what otherwise was an insignificant Florida town.

The first twelve hour race there had been held there in 1952. The track had been laid-out on a deserted, World War II- era airbase- a facility that, when active, had been known as Hendricks Army Airfield. This base had been constructed on 9,200 acres of what had previously been empty, sandy scrubland. Work on it had begun on July 20, 1941, and, amazingly, by today's standards, the initial phase of construction was finished by the end of that same year. But, then an order came from Washington, D.C. to expand the program further so that the facility could be used as the first heavy bomber combat crew training school in the U.S. Later, the field's mission was changed yet again, and it became a specialized school for four-engine bomber pilots.

The base was designed to be a self-supporting city. A rail road spur had been extended to the installation, and the base had paved streets, water and sewage systems, administration buildings, barracks, hangars, four massive runways, and numerous taxiways. Each runway was 300 feet wide and 5,000 feet long. During the war this base proved to be a busy place- training over 10,000 pilots for B-17, B-24, and B-29 aircraft. But, once the war ended the base was no longer necessary. Consequently, it was closed on December 31, 1945, declared surplus, and turned over to the city of Sebring. It had operated as a small, quiet, municipal airport since.

Following the war, as servicemen returned from Europe, they brought with them a fascination for the small, two seat sports cars that they had discovered while stationed there. They also returned with a need for excitement, risk, and danger- conditions to which they had become accustomed during the war. The result was that soon a strong interest in sports car racing swept across America- particularly in the Northeast, and the Upper Midwest. Then, just as today, during the miserable, bone-chilling winter months common to those areas, many of its residents came to Florida to escape the cold and snow to soak in the warmth of the sun. Most of these snowbirds came to golf, or to fish. But, now, some also wanted to continue to embrace their newest passion- racing sports cars. Enter a man named Alec Ulman.

Ulman was a New Yorker. He was also one of the earliest members of the Sports Car Club of America (SCCA), and was friends with many of the most influential members of that organization. Early in his career he had traveled Europe working for several aeronautically focused organizations. Later, during the war, he was President of a company that manufactured landing gear for aircraft. Following the war, having made a fortune, he was able to winter in Florida- socializing with other similarly well heeled, sports car infatuated, snowbirds. In 1950 he attended the Le Mans 24 hour race in France, and returned inspired to organize the first similar American endurance race. Shortly thereafter he had visited the Sebring airbase- looking for space to store surplus aircraft. But, he immediately recognized that the base was a wonderful location at which to hold his dreamed of race. He quickly approached the leaders of the City of Sebring- who jumped at the opportunity to attract some of America's wealthiest citizens to their isolated little village. Wasting no time, Ulman staged the first race at Sebring - a six hour event- on December 31, 1950. Lessons learned from that initial contest led him to reconfigure the event, and the dates on which it would be held. The next race, running for 12 hours, took place on March 15, 1952. It was a huge success.

Ulman and his supporters realized that they had stumbled onto something with immense potential! The nearly mile long runways of the airport allowed drivers to reach the top speeds of their cars, and the roads that wound through the base provided challenging corners to test the vehicles' handling capabilities. Critically, the local municipality was anxious to be helpful- hoping to attract fans to the area. And, the weather in March- during the middle of Spring Break- was absolutely gorgeous. He set about organizing the event for the following year- and began to work diligently to attract exciting entrants. At that latter task he exceeded even his wildest ambitions when England's Aston Martin Company, hoping to sell more cars in the U.S., agreed to enter its two-car factory racing team in the next race. This decision immediately put Sebring on the international sports car racing map. The eventual entry list for the race of fifty nine cars included (besides the Astons) Ferraris, Cunningham's, Jaguar's, Porsche's, Maserati's, OSCA's, MG's, Allard's, and many others. And, when the checkered flag fell at the end of the race the almost unbelievable had happened. An American-built Cunningham had won- defeating the mighty, upper-crust, English Aston Martins. The die had been cast. From then on the world's best sports car racers had to take part in the Sebring 12 Hour race.

Of course, in March, 1953 I was only a little over four years old. I'm pretty sure that that exciting race didn't register in my consciousness. And, of course, I didn't read about it in the Tampa Tribune- the area's premier newspaper. But, as years went past, I most certainly would. The Editor of the paper's sports department had quickly recognized the significance of the race. And, each year dedicated an entire section of the paper to coverage of the race. And, of course, after I learned to read, I devoured every word, and picture, about the race that appeared in the paper. The Tribune's coverage displayed pictures of the amazing cars, interviews with the heroic drivers, and human interest stories about the royalty, the glamorous ladies, and the famous gentlemen who came from all over the world to attend the race. It was very heady stuff for a lad like me. The one thing that I knew for sure was that I had to attend the race- as soon as possible.

My father was neither a car guy, nor a race fan. But, he was a good dad. And, eventually he allowed himself to be talked into taking me to the race in 1963. I was fourteen years old, and I don't think it was possible for any fourteen year old kid to be more excited about anything than I was about going to that race. For weeks, it was all I could think about. But, as you may know, things don't always go smoothly for fourteen year old kids with big plans. And, they didn't go smoothly for me.

At that time I was trying to make my school's junior varsity basketball team. It was late Friday afternoon, the day before the race. We were running laps around the outside asphalt courts that we practiced on. I remember as I ran being so excited that I was going to the race the next day. In fact, while I wasn't a good runner, that day it seemed like I was almost floating on air as I jogged around the perimeter of the court. Perhaps my mind wasn't really on what I was doing. Who knows? But, for whatever reason I managed to step off the edge of the pavement with my right foot, spraining my ankle worse than I had ever done. Initially, I thought that I had broken my ankle. My first worry was whether I could get it set in time to and be able to still go to the race in the morning. I didn't cry, but damn, I wanted to. Somehow, I eventually managed to bike home, where Mom helped me soak my ankle in hot water and Epson Salts (that's what you did back then). I think afterwards that she may have wrapped it for me, too. I was absolutely determined that there was no way I was going to miss going to the race.

The other issue that had to be dealt with was something that to this day still bothers me. At that time, I was in the school band- I played a trumpet in the horn section. Unfortunately, the school had been invited, on the morning of the race, to have its band play for the grand opening of a nearby, newly expanded phosphate processing plant. I had known about this conflict for weeks, and had tried my best to get out of having to attend the concert. But, for whatever reason, the bandmaster wouldn't agree to let me miss the event. He finally told me that if I didn't show up he would kick me out of the band! Jeez! Clearly he didn't understand how important this race was to me. Dad, dutifully, delivered me, attired in my band uniform, to the plant at the specified time- it seems like it was at ten o'clock. As soon as all the speeches were over, and the band had been dismissed, I ran to the car, changed out of my band uniform, and we left for the track.

We arrived at the track sometime around one in the afternoon. But, even though the race had been going on for hours the race's record crowd meant that we still had to wait in traffic before we could finally enter the gate. To me, that delay, was excruciating. Then, to add insult to injury, once inside, we had to inch along at a snail's pace as fans wandered steadily (and unsteadily) across the road in front of the car. I remember Dad not being amused by their meanderings. Eventually, we were able to find a parking spot in the vicinity of Turn One, and walked to a viewing area alongside the track.

In those days the track's first turn was a high speed bend to the left-taken at, or nearly at, full speed. Spectators were separated, at a distance of several hundred feet, from the cars on the track by a flimsy stretch of "snow fence." And, already much of that fencing had been knocked to the ground by the press of eager fans leaning against it. That, of course, was okay for me. We stood on that spot, me on my painful ankle, for the remaining eight hours of the race. Mom had made us some sandwiches, and we had a cooler full of cokes (sodas, or pop, to those of you from up north).

I still have many vivid memories from that first race. One is of the smell that the cars produced. At that time, some of the engine oils that many of the teams used contained castor oil in their formulations, and as the engines burned that oil during the race it created a pungent, but not unpleasant, aroma that hung in the atmosphere around the track. I thought that was cool. In my mind I can still smell it.

Another memory is of the sounds that the car's made. It didn't take long to discover that the engines of these cars didn't sound at all like the engines I was used to. The Jaguar engines were straight sixes, and their notes were sweet, and pure. The Porsches had opposed fours, and their engines sounded raspy, and blatant, but, still, aggressive. The American Corvettes, and Cobras, featured large capacity V-8s, with exhaust notes that were deep throated, powerful, and loud- just as I had expected. But, clearly the most memorable sounds were those made by the many V-12-engined Ferraris. It was a sound that was distinctive- a piercing, higher-pitched, more complicated, almost ripping, scream. But, yet this noise managed, somehow, at the same time, to also be almost melodic- a wondrous mechanical cacophony that I have never quite forgotten.

But, these exhaust notes weren't the only noises to be heard. Joining in were the squealing of brakes as they desperately scraped off speed. And, these were followed by the tortured screaming of tires as the cars sped around the following twist in the course. Occasionally, we would then hear a louder howl, as a car left the track, its tires having lost their struggle for friction. These episodes focused everyone's attention- our heads always turned towards the sound to anxiously listen for a thud- the sickening notice that that slide had caused a crash. Added to that was a random percussion of exhaust backfires. In time, all of these noises blended together and created a marvelous, harmonic symphony- a composition which, in my mind, would have left Debussy and Copeland envious.

Another recollection has to do with the beautiful shapes and resplendent colors of the cars. The svelte Jaguars were white, with dark blue racing stripes running down the center of the cars- Briggs Cunningham's traditional team colors. The bullet-like Porsches were generally, in the Germanic tradition, silver. But, clearly the most spectacular of all were the stunning Ferrari GTOs. These front- engine coupes, with bodies so beautiful and sinuous that they produced an almost sexual desire, were tinted in multiple stunning hues. I remember that several wore different shades of metallic blue, one glittered in a deep metallic green, while a couple of were painted in classic, Italian red.

And, of course, there were also the Ferrari prototypes that were leading the race. They - in every possible way- were in a league of their own. They were faster, quicker, and more spectacular, as they easily passed other cars. By the time we arrived three of these cars were contesting the overall lead. Two were brand new, rear- engine "250Ps," entered by the Ferrari factory in the cars' debut race. The other was an older front-engine Testa Rossa, entered by Luigi Chinetti's North American Racing Team (NART). This car was powered by the largest V-12 engine that Ferrari had ever raced. This brute had been designed specifically to win the previous year's Le Mans 24 hour race- a feat it had easily accomplished. But, now it was simply last year's car, having essentially been made obsolete by the factory's decision to race V-12 motors in its rear-engine cars. Consequently, this "dinosaur" of a car had been handed down to the NART team- a decidedly second level operation- to see what success it might still be able to achieve.

Driving the factory Ferrari cars were the team's top level factory hot shoes: England's motorcycle, and soon to be F1, world champion, John Surtees; Italian Lodovico Scarfiotti; Sicilian racer, and law professor, Nino Vacarella; future F1 driver Lorenzo Bandini; and the wild Belgian, Willy Mairesse. Driving the older, but still spectacular, NART-entered car were Britain's mustachioed, dry-witted, 1962 Formula One World Champion, Graham Hill; and the quick, young Mexican firebrand, Pedro Rodriquez-who was making his return to racing following the death of his younger, even more tempestuous, and quicker, brother Ricardo, who had died tragically in his home town of Mexico City while practicing for the last Formula One race of the previous season.

Given the overwhelming impressions made by the splendid machinery that was speeding by, it was easy, at first, to overlook the human struggle taking place. But, as time went by I began to pull for Hill and Rodriquez. They were the underdogs- racing an older car- up against a full factory-supported effort. They were clearly not supposed to win. But, surprisingly, by the time we had arrived they had led almost the entire race, and, as the afternoon went on, their lead had grown to three laps. As this lead built we could sense a growing frustration on the part of the factory cars' drivers. As we watched, they had begun to push harder, brake later, slide wider, and drive more aggressively as they sliced past slower traffic. Clearly they wanted to avoid being embarrassed by last year's car. We could sense that they were starting to take greater and greater risks- risks that exposed them, not only to spinning off the track and possibly falling out of the race, but also to an increased likelihood of injury, or even death. What I was watching now had become more than just a rapid parade of beautiful, spectacular cars- it was now becoming a life or death struggle- a contest in which grown men were willingly placing their very existence on the line of sporting challenge. It was truly an enthralling spectacle. (As evidence that this was not simply hyperbole, of the seven men driving the top three cars- only one would be able to retire from racing without having either been killed, or having suffered extremely serious injuries.)

As I took this in, I questioned whether what I was enjoying was in some ways no different, and no better, than when Roman gladiators fought the lions, or when matadors danced with bulls. But, yet, somehow, this seemed different. Of course, I didn't want to see anyone injured. Still, I thrilled at the thought of brave men pushing the limits of physics. This wasn't animal against animal, or muscle against muscle, it- or so I reasoned- was man, and his intellect, challenging the very forces of nature. This, to me, somehow, seemed important.

As the sun began to set, despite the increasingly heroic efforts of the factory drivers, the older car still held a comfortable lead. A major upset was in the works. It seemed like the whole crowd now was cheering for the Testa Rossa to stay in front. But, as darkness covered the track, problems began for the front-engine Ferrari. As the driver turned on the car's headlights it became obvious that there was some kind of electrical problem with the car since its lights were not nearly as bright as they should have been. Then, as the car continued to speed lap after lap around the course, we could see the beams growing dimmer and dimmer. Eventually, the car's bulbs were producing only a faint glow. Graham Hill, doing his best to negotiate the now dark track, was still trying desperately to hold on to the lead. At some points, I recall, he resorted to following slower cars, using their headlights to see the darkest, almost invisible, parts of the track. Inevitably, despite these heroic efforts, the factory cars began to close. Finally, the officials black flagged the Testa Rossa for insufficient illumination, forcing it into the pits. The problem was with the car's alternator- it was not producing enough current to both fire the engine and power the lights- with the alternator out of commission the car had been running only on the current from its battery. The team knew that it couldn't change the alternator without losing too much time. So, instead, it decided to turn off the car's lights, change the car's battery to power the engine, and to satisfy the requirements for lighting, it simply taped flashlights onto the Testa Rossa's front and rear fenders. With those quick fixes made, the big brute of a car roared back onto the track- this time with Rodriquez behind the wheel. But, now he was a lap behind the factory cars- trying desperately to chase them down. Slowly, despite having essentially no driving lights, he unbelievably began to reel the factory racers in. But, over time, the beating that he was subjecting the older car to began to take its toll. We noticed that the car's exhaust pipe had come loose, and it was now dragging beneath the speeding Ferrari. This, in the pitch black night, created a shower of brilliant sparks as the car roared around the track. I still vividly recall the sight of this virtual comet speeding down the long back stretch- the streaming fireworks, and the screaming bellow of the un-muffled V-12 engine, the only way that spectators could know that Rodriquez was still desperately chasing down the cars in front. But, eventually, it became too much, even for Rodriquez. The combination of no lights, and engine problems caused by not having an exhaust system, meant that the chase became a lost cause. Then, only after all chances of victory for the NART car had disappeared, did the officials notice that that car may also not have had any functioning brake lights. Luigi Chinetti, as I remember hearing described over the track's loud speakers, engaged the race's chief steward in a forceful debate in the pits about whether this observation was true or not. Apparently, Chinetti won the argument as the car was allowed to stay on the track until the end of the race.

Eventually, all of this drama played itself out, and the Surtees/ Scarfiotti Ferrari won the race- one lap ahead of its sister car, and two laps ahead of the car that I had been cheering for. I was beside myself with excitement. Then, as the last of the cars entered the pits, and the track- our ears now aching from the sudden cessation of noise- became silent, we drug our gear back to the car, and climbed in for the late, long trip home. I was already beginning to stress about how I could possibly manage to survive the next twelve months before I would again be able to attend this race when my Dad did something totally unexpected. The road that led out of the track passed alongside the track's front straight, and the pits were located parallel to that. As we drove by we could see the victory stand where the winners were being celebrated, and we could hear the public address announcers enthusiastically congratulating them. That's when Dad did what I thought was totally out of character. He pulled the car to the side of the road, and said: "Let's see if we can get in."

Fortunately, the crowd that had wanted into the pits after the race had done a great job of pushing down the fencing, and all we had to do was walk right onto the track. I was surprised that no one seemed to care. Soon, my aching ankle forgotten, I was standing beside the raised platform where the victory celebrations were taking place. The overall winners, by this time, were gone, and now the announcers were making awards to the winners in the smaller car classes. Truthfully, I didn't care much about that.

But, what I did care greatly about was that the winning open-topped Ferrari 250P was still parked in front of victory lane. It drew me towards it- like a magnet. I could finally see the car up close; I could touch it; I could even smell it! By this time I was standing beside the driver's door, so close that I could look down directly into the cockpit. I noticed that there were two seats, with the driver's seat on the right. I was surprised to see that the seats were upholstered only in a plain, sweat- stained, medium-blue cotton cloth- I guess I had been expecting to see expensive leather in such a fantastic, world beating vehicle. Later, I learned that this fabric was standard for Ferrari's racing cars. The legend claimed that this simple cloth covering had become a Ferrari tradition when, while in a desperate late night thrash as mechanics frantically prepared the car for the company's first race, the team, in desperation, resorted to using this simple blue cloth to upholster the seats . Where did the team source that material? The story is that one of the mechanics donated his overalls.

Whether that claim is fact, or fiction, I can't say. But, given frequent experiences during my racing career of similar late-night attempts to ready a car for the next day's race, this tale certainly has the ring of authenticity.

Another surprise, upon peering further into the cockpit, was at just how Spartan everything was. The dash, for example, was just a flat, painted piece of sheet metal. I had expected more. And, on that dash were only three gauges: a tachometer being the largest and most prominent; and on either side were simple water temperature and oil pressure gauges. There were a couple of switches, and a starter button. But, that was it. Simple stuff- only the minimal amount required for the job at hand. Somehow, I found that comforting. I was pretty certain that, if given the opportunity, I would have been able to drive that car. And, with the certainty of youth, I was sure that, with a little practice, I could have driven it as quickly as John Surtees had.

To the right of the driver's seat was the gear shift. It looked just like I'd read in the magazines that it should look. It was nothing more than a simple, strong, machined, and polished metal gate, with corners slightly rounded to smooth the lever's rapid transitions from one gear to another. I was happy to confirm that the car had a five speed transmission- with its shift pattern laid out in, what I had read, was the classic racing tradition. First gear was located on the far left, and down- out of the way. I knew that it would normally only be used either when starting a race, or coming out of the pits. There was no question that I would be able to shift the gears in this car when the opportunity presented itself.

The final thing I noticed, nestled between the right side of the seat and the transmission shift mechanism, was a simple rubber cup. And, in that cup were segments of oranges- probably having come from one of the nearby groves that surrounded the track. Some of these segments had been sucked dry; others were as yet unused. Obviously, this was how the drivers had replenished themselves during the race. And, that was comforting, too- I liked oranges.

I could have stood there all night, but soon I had to step away as a group of brown overall clad Italian mechanics began to push the car away. As I watched the car roll down the pit lane I heard Dad suggest that it was time for us to go, too.

Chapter Four: Practicing

I took a number of understandings away from that race at Sebring. First, people- real people, who didn't appear to be fundamentally different from me- actually raced the cars that up to this point I'd only read, and dreamed, about. Second, an important part of this racing activity took place in my very own neighborhood. It wasn't like this phenomenal stuff only happened in the exotic locales of Europe. And, third, I'd confirmed, with my own eyes, there was nothing about this foreign machinery that I couldn't understand, and operate. Heck, from what I'd seen, they were really not that much different from the grove tractors that I'd already been driving. Therefore, the conclusion I reached from these observations was that I could, easily enough, do what I'd seen these other fellows doing on the track. I knew that I'd, of course, need a little practice, and, besides, I wasn't yet old enough to have a go. But, I knew now that I could do this. And, that, eventually, I would. Heck- this was America in the 1960's- everything was possible.

From that point on I began to prepare for my eventual, inevitable, sports car racing career.

Unfortunately, of course, at that point I didn't yet have a car of my own to drive. But, I figured that if I played my cards right, Dad would probably help me get a car of some kind as soon as I turned sixteen. In the meantime, I could start to get ready- reading and studying as much as possible about driving and racing, and driving whatever, whenever, I could.

The first part of my plan was to explore what books might be available in the school's library about automobile racing. Unfortunately, regardless of how many times I flipped through the cards in the library's files, there just wasn't that much to be found. The only thing that I could come up with was a series of fiction books about sports car racing. In these tales the books protagonist took on the world's best drivers in his American-built special- 'The Black Tiger.' It didn't take me long to devour those stories. They weren't exactly what I had been looking for, but they did help strengthen my conviction that an American- with talent, and hard work- could achieve what I wanted to achieve. So far, so good. But, I knew that I needed more- so I began to look in the magazines to see what else might be available. It didn't take long to focus on the ads for the automotive-focused book stores. And, soon I found what I had been looking for- a text book on sports car racing. The book I had found was entitled *"The Technique of Motor Racing"* by Piero Taruffi. It certainly sounded promising. I knew that Taruffi was, or at least had been, a very successful Italian racing driver. He'd even driven for Ferrari, and I knew that he'd won the legendary Mille Miglia, a thousand mile, non-stop race through the roads of Italy. After that victory, he'd honored the promise he'd made to his wife before the race that he'd retire from racing if he was able to come home victorious. I told Mom that this book was what I'd like for that year's Christmas. But, Christmas, unfortunately, was still months away.

But, I did what I could do. I'd read enough in the magazines to understand some of the techniques involved in racing. So, I began to practice developing those skills. I, of course, didn't yet have a car, but I did have a bicycle. Therefore, it was possible to apply what I was learning, and often I would ride for hours around the streets of the neighborhood, experimenting with different lines through the corners and turns. I often practiced recognizing the apex of corners- then I would modify my line to understand how apexing later, or earlier, would impact speed through the corners. I even remember timing myself around a two-block long track that I'd laid out, seeing how my lap times would be impacted using different lines. What the heck- I was a kid, with lots of time on my hands.

When I'd grow tired of riding around those same two blocks I'd sometimes draw, using a rock as a crayon, a course on the paved road in front of my house, and then race through it. While to the uninitiated it might have looked like all I was doing was aimlessly driving around in circles, in actuality I was trying to learn what lines would work best through the various types of corners. For example, I leaned that in a constant radius corner a mid-corner apex point was proper. But, a decreasing radius turn required the use of a later apex. Conversely, an early apex could be used if the corner opened up on exit. I also learned that sometimes a complex of corners might require compromising the ideal line in one or more portions of the turns so that a proper line could be used in the more important exit sector. This really was not a silly exercise. I was learning good stuff. Stuff that I would eventually apply throughout my racing career.

But, I needed that book! I knew that there was so much more that I needed to learn. It was tough waiting until Christmas. But, finally that day arrived. I remember anxiously unwrapping presents until I finally found what I really wanted. Then I was over the moon with excitement. As soon as I was able I excused myself, I went into a bedroom where I would have the quiet needed to read and concentrate. I seemed to remember that I didn't come out of the bedroom until Mom called me that night for dinner!

The book was everything that I thought it would be, and more. Not only was Taruffi a gifted, experienced, and accomplished racer- he also had a PhD in Engineering. Initially, I was taken aback to find that the book was filled with graphs, charts, and formulas. In other words, it was loaded with math- and pretty high powered math, at that!!!! Who knew that racers had to know all this stuff? This part was not exactly what I had been expecting. So I decided that for my first pass through the book I'd just look at the pictures- and it was loaded with super cool photos. But, eventually, I made the decision to jump into the text to see what I could learn.

I was delighted to discover that the book's foreword was written by none other than Juan Manuel Fangio- 5 time World's Driving champion! I knew that there was no one in racing any bigger, any more legendary, than Fangio. I was delighted. And, even more pleased to see that, in the first paragraph, Fangio declared that this was the first book that had been written for drivers- "a textbook on motor racing"- exactly what I had been looking for. I also learned that Taruffi had accomplished much more in racing than I had previously realized. As a young man he had raced motorcycles, and eventually had won the European Championship. Then, after the war, he had turned his attention to four -wheel racing with a great deal of success-winning almost all of the legendary open road endurance races including Mexico's Carerra Panamerica, and Sicily's Targa Florio. Fangio's parting comments were "a young driver's progress will be greatly assisted by taking his (Taruffi's) advice, and absorbing all he has to say.... The rest lies in a man's own personal make-up- those peculiar, intangible assets of mind and body which no text book can describe, no formula resolve, but which provide the final inspiration....the stock-in trade of the great driver."

I found all of this to be somehow encouraging. I knew that I'd eventually be able to read, understand, and comprehend everything that was in the book. And, I found it to be comforting that an educated and intellectual man like Taruffi could enjoy and accomplish so much in racing. The fact that racing and academic accomplishments were not incompatible relieved my mind a great deal. Now, as to whether I actually possessed the peculiar assets of mind and body that Fangio mentioned I wasn't sure. I already knew that I wasn't a great athlete, but I thought my mind was probably okay. Hopefully, it would help to overcome whatever attributes that I might lack physically.

In the book's first chapter, Taruffi described the five "Necessary Qualities" that a driver must possess if he is to obtain reasonable results. These were:

1. Great enthusiasm.
2. A sizeable helping of courage, and mastery over his nerves.
3. The right mental and physical make-up.
4. Physical fitness and lots of stamina.
5. A good bank balance.

There, obviously, was no problem with me meeting the first requirement! But, I wasn't sure about the second requirement for courage and nerves. I had to grade that, at this point, as an unknown. I figured that I was okay with the mental part. However, my honest review of the physical requirement was somewhat mixed. I'd always been a stocky, overweight kid, who wasn't particularly good at running or jumping. And, I wasn't particularly good either at hitting a baseball, or shooting baskets. By this time I'd already realized that I was never going to be a star in any of the stick and ball sports. But, I did play football- so I was reasonably fit. And, I thought I had a reasonable degree of stamina. But, the fifth requirement was one I clearly recognized as potentially being an issue. As a fourteen year old kid I didn't have a bank account! Heck, even my 'piggy bank' was empty. And, my family, while comfortable, was very far from being wealthy. But, finally, I decided that any driver with as much talent as I obviously possessed would eventually be able to attract the funding necessary to go racing. And, if that didn't work, I could always do it the hard way by working, and earning, what I needed.

Bottom line- even though I only clearly met roughly half of Taruffi's requirements- I concluded that I satisfied enough of them to reasonably expect some level of future success. And, besides, maybe I would be able to meet more of them after I grew up. I remember, after going through this analysis, being a little disappointed that it wasn't obvious that I already possessed everything that would be needed to become an automobile racing champion. But, after this simple analysis, while it was already obvious that getting to the top step of the victory podium would not be easy, it was, at least, theoretically, possible. And, to me, that was enough.

Let's go racing!

Book Two: *Dies Irae*

What trembling there will be

When the judge shall come

To weigh everything strictly!

Chapter Five: My First Racing Experiences

After having read Taruffis's book, I was obviously now well qualified. I was sure that all I needed at this point, in order to develop my racing skills to a world class level, was practice. And, I tried to do that. I tried to practice applying what I had learned to every activity that I participated in.

For example, walking the hallways and sidewalks at school presented great opportunities for identifying proper corner apexes. And, unsurprisingly, I didn't see anything unusual about that! Hah!

My bicycle, of course, remained the primary tool for furthering my driving education. And, I can still remember quite clearly a few of the more important lessons I learned with it. Once, when using a gas station's air hose to ensure that the tires on my bicycle were inflated to a proper pressure for racing, I managed to explode one of the bike's Dunlop's in my face. That was a heck of pop! The lesson I learned was to always pay attention to the maximum inflation pressures specified for the tire. And, to always use a tire pressure gauge.

Another bicycle memory came from an early experimentation with speed. Near my house, the town's high school stood on top of a sizeable ridge. And, the road that left the school exited down a long, steep slope. A perfect stretch of "track," I reasoned, on which to improve my high speed driving skills. I had practiced this exercise, without incident, for a number of weekends. And, with each of these successes, I reasoned that my inherent latent abilities to handle high speeds were making themselves increasingly obvious. This illusion, however, was not to last long.

I remember that that particular morning was absolutely glorious- one of those delightfully cooler, lower humidity days in Florida that follow the passage of overnight cold fronts- fronts accompanied by heavy rain storms. Perfect conditions, I reasoned, for trying to go really fast on my bicycle. I was almost down the test track's hill, moving quicker than I had ever gone before, when it realized that I might have a wee bit of a problem. The previous night's heavy rain had deposited several inches of loose sand and dirt at the base of the hill. But, unfortunately, I didn't have time to react. In an instant my front tire dug into that debris, and still moving at a very considerable speed, I was thrown over the handle bars of the bike. Fortunately, I didn't land on my head- In those days, no one wore helmets. Instead, I came down on my left calf- there was no dirt where I landed. Rather, I fell on a section of rough asphalt that had been washed clean by the storm. I learned that day about road rash. Much of the skin on the top, and side, of my lower left leg was scraped away. When I finally stopped tumbling, and looked at the injury, I thought that, literally, I could see meat and muscle. It was not a pretty site. And, my bike was hurt almost as badly as I was. I knew that I would have to straighten it before I could even think about riding home- walking, clearly, was not an option. But, attempting that repair would have to wait until I could deal with the pain, and stand.

Thankfully, the hurting eventually lessened, and I was able to straighten the bike's wheel enough to slowly pedal home. Fortunately, neither Mom nor Dad was there when I arrived. So I applied first aid on my own- I started with soap and water- trying to wash out all the embedded sand and pebbles. I followed that up with a liberal application of hydrogen peroxide, reasoning that the resulting bubbles would lift out any remaining grit. Then I topped off the wound with cotton pads, gauze and tape. When Mom came home I casually explained that I had fallen off the bike after it had slid on some sand (technically, the truth). I tried to minimize the extent of the injury, not wanting to admit my stupidity. I have carried the resulting scar since.

Some of the conclusions that I reached, after having thought this incident through, were:

- Too much courage can get you trouble.
- There was a remote possibility that I might not have quite as much skill and talent as I had previously assumed.
- And, you can actually get hurt doing this stuff.

But, none of these served, in the least, to diminish my desire to become a great automobile racer. If anything, I considered these, and similar episodes, as just being the necessary dues that all aspiring drivers had to pay. Dues, which in time, would probably make me tougher on the track. This episode did, however, serve to completely erase any desire to ever want to ride motorcycles!

Unfortunately, it wasn't long before I would learn another lesson. I was, of course, still too young to legally drive a car on the road, but there was no law against me driving in the middle of a cow pasture. My Dad and Uncle, at that time, jointly owned a section of rural land on which they were raising cattle, and growing oranges. I went with Dad on most weekends to help with those endeavors. Fortunately, Dad would sometimes, when my help was not otherwise required, let me drive one of the farm's trucks around the field. My favorite vehicle to drive was the big "cow truck." This big Chevy was called that because it was what we used to transport cattle whenever they needed to be moved from pasture to pasture, or be carried to the market. On the back frame of the truck was mounted a wide flat wooden floor with tall, strong metal cattle fencing, and sliding entry door, surrounding that. Critically to this tale, this flooring and structure was slightly wider than the fenders of the truck-protruding on each side by roughly a foot.

I thought that this big truck was really cool to drive because it had a "four on the floor" transmission, or at least a cow truck's version of such. For those who may be unfamiliar with the lingo of the time, having a "four on the floor" meant that a vehicle was equipped with a transmission with four forward speeds, and with a shift lever that stuck up from the floor comfortably close to the driver's right hand. While this arrangement in trucks was common, in car's it was perceived as being much sportier than the more common "three on the tree"- a derogatory term which meant that the vehicle had only a three speed transmission that was operated by a slow, difficult, balky steering column-mounted shift lever. Critically to me, sports cars of that time usually had the "four on the floor" arrangement. Granted, there were some huge differences between a sports car and a cow truck, but to a wide-eyed kid like me those discrepancies didn't seem all that significant. I could still practice shifting gears, and much more importantly, I could practice "heeling and toeing" as I downshifted from one gear into the next.

Of course, I could also practice identifying the apex of corners as I happily steered the big truck around corners. I should mention two things at this time: first, I probably never went faster than fifteen or twenty miles per hour; and second, there weren't that many corners in the pasture. In fact, the only one that I really had to deal with was a right-angled corner of barbed wire fencing. We (my dad, my uncle, my cousin, and me) had recently spent several weekends building this fence around a soon to be planted orange grove, and it represented a considerable investment of time, effort, sweat, and money. It looked good, and we were all justifiably proud of it.

But, still, to me, the angle of that fence represented a corner- a corner with a clear apex point. And, one of the things I had learned from reading Taruffi's book was that it was critically important to always clip your apex points as closely as possible. I had learned that any gap from the ideal point created a shortening of the maximum corner radius, and that such a departure from the ideal always resulted in a lowering of the theoretical maximum speed (thank you Piero Taruffi) at which a corner could be taken. Obviously, it was critical to practice clipping your apexes closely.

Unfortunately, in my zeal to leave little space between the side of the truck and the apex point (i.e., the fence's big, strong, critically important corner post), I had forgotten that the flooring on the back of the truck protruded twelve inches beyond the side of the truck. But, I was quickly reminded of this fact when the truck's bed slammed into this post and shuddered to an immediate stop. I quickly backed away from the post, and jumped out to see how much damage I had done. I was delighted to see no obvious damage to the truck. I was just beginning to think that I had gotten away with doing really something stupid, when I looked at the fence. Then, my heart fell. What had previously been a straight, perfectly vertical corner post that anchored a half mile of tight barbed wire in each direction was now leaning over at a 45 degree angle- broken off at the ground. The barbed wire, which had previously stretched taughtly towards the horizon, now lazily sagged towards the ground. I knew that I was in trouble. Big trouble! That fence would have to be repaired.

I slowly drove across the pasture, not in any hurry to fess up to what I had done, to where the crew was finishing what it had been working on. I honestly reported what had happened, and we all drove together to inspect the damage. We then spent a couple of hours, hours beyond our normal quitting time, re-setting a new corner post, re-stretching the barber wire, and re-stapling the wire to the fence posts. This repair made for a very long day, especially for me. Throughout it, I had to endure many well-earned critiques of my driving ability, each followed by loud guffaws, and laughter. Lessons learned? Be careful. And, when you drive think about what you're doing.

But, despite these setbacks, my enthusiasm, and desire, remained as strong as ever. Happily, it wasn't long before the State of Florida, in its wisdom, issued me a Learner's Permit, a restricted driver's license that allowed me to drive a car on the road, as long as one of my parents was seated in the passenger's seat.

The family car was a long, nine-passenger, six-cylinder, Chevy station wagon. It featured, of course, the dreaded "three on the tree." Despite my appetite for going fast, I never attempted to drive above the speed limit, understanding well that doing this would certainly lead to me being banned from driving by my parents, and possibly lead to, horror of horrors, losing my license. But, still I was soon happy to demonstrate for my parents some of the new higher level driving techniques I had learned in the book. And one of the things of I was most proud was my ability to heel and toe, while performing double clutch downshifts. This, of course, was not all that easy given the Chevy's very widely spaced clutch, brake, and accelerator pedals. But, with practice it could be done.

Another shortcoming of the car was its aforementioned three speed transmission- whose gear ratios were, necessarily, widely spaced. This spacing made it difficult to smoothly match the speeds of the transmission and engine as I tried to rapidly shift down from third to second gears. Dad, as I remember, was not impressed, expressing some concern about the damage that I might be causing the engine. I tried to assure him that I knew what I was doing, and that besides, after all, I was saving wear and tear on the brakes. I remember him mumbling something, possibly obscene, under his breath. But, he let me keep driving. And, Mom, bless her soul, never seemed to mind.

Chapter Six: A Car of My Own

Any boy's senior year in high school is always a memorable time. Certainly, mine, in 1966, was- for many, many reasons- not the least of which was that my Dad had bought me a car! I couldn't believe it: this "Aspiring World's Greatest Racing Driver" now had his very own set of "wheels."

It wasn't, of course, a new car- but, that didn't bother me- not in the least. I was just ecstatic to have any car at all! I can imagine the anguish that my parents must have gone through when trying to decide whether they should make this purchase. I'm sure the thought that I could easily kill myself, and others, once I got behind the wheel had to have crossed their minds more than once. But, on the other hand, I know that they had to have been tired of hauling an active teenage boy around. In the end, a friend of my Dad's sealed the deal with an extremely attractive offer.

This friend was in the scrap metal business- in fact, he'd become very wealthy taking unwanted scrap metal off the hands of the area's phosphate mines, and then recycling it. He may have recycled used cars, too. Regardless, for some reason, he'd acquired a low mileage, pristine 1959 Renault Dauphine, and subsequently sold it to my Dad for only $250. I'm sure to my parents it looked like the perfect vehicle for their speed crazed young son- after all, it only had 30 horsepower! And, the specs said that the car's 0-60 time was unbelievably slow- 32 seconds. In fact, Time Magazine, in naming it one of the 50 worst cars of all time, said that it had a "rate of acceleration that you could measure with a calendar...." One would be excused for thinking that a young man like me, in the middle of the 1960's- a period known today as the "Muscle Car Era"- would have been disappointed with this acquisition. After all, one of my friends was driving a Chevy Malibu with a four on the floor, and a

4-barrel, 350 cubic inch V-8; and another guy that we knew actually had a Dodge Hemi! But, you would have been wrong. I'm sure to my parents' confusion and dismay, I was actually over the moon about this car. The reason why-? I knew some stuff about this car that they didn't know!

For example, I had read that a Dauphine had actually won the 1958 Monte Carlo Rally, and after that, the Tour de Corse. And, in 1959, the model had been victorious in the Coupes de Alpes, the Rallye de Cote d'Ivorie, and the Liege-Rome-Liege Rally. It had, in truth, established itself as an extremely competent rally car. Granted, those wins had been achieved with cars that had been extensively modified by the legendary tuner of Renaults-the so-called "Wizard," Amedee Gordini. But, still- it was essentially, the same car that I was now driving. Further, I remembered that the Dauphine had also distinguished itself at Sebring, the track that I literally worshipped- it had won its class there in 1957! So- not only did I now have a rally champion, I had a winning racing car, too. Clearly, I was now on my way to the top!

For those who may not remember, I'll take a few moments to describe this vehicle. It was a four door, rear-engined, economy car that had been designed to compete with the Volkswagen Beetle. Its engine was 845 cc in capacity, which was mated to a floor-mounted, three speed transmission. (Not quite a 'four on the floor' but close enough.) Its chassis was also exciting because it featured "monococoque" construction, i.e., longitudinal box sections with cross bracing- which was essentially the same design concept just then coming into vogue in the mid-1960's Formula One cars! And, it featured independent suspension on all four wheels- a far superior arrangement to the solid axles then found on almost all American vehicles. Granted, the rear suspension used swing arms- which allegedly could contribute to over steer- but, this design been created by none other than Ferdinand Porsche. And, did I mention that the engine was mounted behind the rear wheels- just like Porsche had done on his own cars. To my way of thinking this thing was practically an inexpensive, high-tech, exotic car, albeit without much in the way of horsepower. But, surely, my driving talent could make up for whatever it lacked in that regard!

Chapter Seven: Select Renault Dauphine Driving Experiences

Adventures in Over Steer:

The aforementioned swing axle suspension in the Renault was one of its most distinguishing features. This design allowed the rear wheels to react independently to irregularities in the pavement's surface, and consequently enabled the vehicle, within limits, to enjoy comfortable, and secure, road holding. The design's name derived from the fact that each axle was connected to the differential by a universal joint- with no universal joint at the wheels. Consequently, the wheels always moved perpendicularly to the drive shafts. The advantage of this arrangement was that it reduced unsprung weight in the suspension, and it eliminated sympathetic camber changes in the opposite wheel. But, the design could also produce a great amount of single-wheel camber change- since the wheel always had to be perpendicular to the axle- and, this camber change could lead, under heavy cornering loads, to a reduction in cornering force by the rear tires and ultimately to a condition known as oversteer, i.e., a condition where the car turns by more than the amount commanded by the driver. In the extreme, this could cause a car to actually spin, as the back of the car tried to rotate around its front wheels.

To reduce this tendency Renault had thoughtfully fitted the car with a front anti-roll bar, and had specified a significant tire pressure differential, which called for lower pressure in the front tires and higher pressure in the rears. But, as I soon discovered, the manufacturer's efforts to limit this condition were not entirely successful. In fact, it was still relatively easy, with enough speed, and with enough aggressive steering input, to generate a significant amount of over steer. And, soon, that was how I went around corners whenever conditions allowed- with the tail end of the car hung out at a significant angle, while I casually steered the front tires to catch the slide. Truthfully, it was relatively easy to do, and I never did actually spin that car out completely. And, I learned to enjoy going sideways. But, many of my passengers- especially those in the rear seat, probably didn't enjoy the experience as much as I did.

Conquering the Rally World:

I lived in Polk County, Florida. (For some unknown reason, the marketing minds in the county then always referred to it as "Imperial Polk County." I guess they were simply trying to do whatever they could to make it sound more important, and more interesting, than it actually was.) Early in my developing driving career I was fortunate to have discovered an organization known as the "Imperial Polk County Sports Car Club." If my memory serves me correctly, I stumbled upon this group as the family was driving home from a visit to the grandparents on a quiet Sunday afternoon along a road that ran parallel to what was, usually, a perpetually dormant municipal airport on Lakeland's north side. But, on that day, much to my surprise, a portion of the field was jammed with dozens of expensive looking sports cars, some of which were actually speeding around cones that marked out a tight, twisting circuit. Dad, with Mom's encouragement, acquiesced to my screeching entreaties that we stop, watch and explore what was going on.

And, what was going on was what was then referred to as a "gymkhana." The goal of the event was for drivers to get through the marked out course in the shortest possible time and with the fewest mistakes (you incurred time penalties for knocking over cones). We soon learned that there were different classes for all types of cars. In other words, you didn't have to own an actual sport car to enter- even Volkswagen Beetles and Renault Dauphines could race. I seem to remember being more excited to learn that information than Dad and Mom were. But, I figured that that was only to be expected.

I also learned that the Club sponsored rally events. These contests were of the TSD (time, speed, distance), or regularity, variety in which contestants drove each segment of a specified course on a public highway in a specified time at a specified average legal speed. Each entry usually competed as a team which consisted of both a driver and a navigator. The team who finished closest to the calculated perfect time was the winner. That sounded simple enough, and given the rally pedigree of my new car, it sounded like something at which I should be able to excel. It also sounded sort of like the legendary Mille Miglia that my driving book's author, Piero Taruffi, had won. This was something that I knew I had to do.

Of course, the first order of business was to find a like minded soul to serve as a navigator. Truthfully, these events were really designed to allow couples to spend a fun afternoon together in a car. But, at that time, that thought simply never crossed my mind. Primarily that was because I didn't know any girls who actually liked cars. And, perhaps even more importantly, I didn't know any girls who actually liked me. Besides, I was in it to win it. I needed a real navigator- a guy able to both read, and more importantly, do mathematical calculations as he bounced along in the passenger seat. Fortunately, I knew just the right guy.

I had played ball with Wayne Johns since I had started to play ball. Granted, he actually played ball a lot better than I did- he was the star quarterback, pitcher, and a basketball phenom. Let's just say that, athletically, I wasn't any of those things. But, despite that we'd always been friends. Wayne was also very gifted at math. As evidence of that he planned, after graduation, to attend Georgia Tech to become an engineer (which he subsequently did). Hell, he even had a slide rule, and knew how to use it! And, he liked cars, too. He was the perfect guy for the job. We entered the next rally.

My recollection of this is somewhat hazy. I seem to recall that it began near a sports car repair garage on the Lakeland's western side. In these events you were given only moments before you were dispatched with a package of instructions that specified an average speed to be maintained for each segment, along with detailed instructions for where to go. Such things as: "Proceed for .25 miles, turn left." That guidance would be followed by "Proceed for 3.6 miles, and bear slightly right." And, so on. The average speed that was specified was always below the average legal speed for the entire segment. For example, if the average legal speed limit for the segment was 55 miles per hour, the specified speed might be 48 miles per hour. No reason to ever speed- right? Ha! Throw in the effect of stopping and starting at stop signs and red lights. And, given the potential consequence of making the occasional wrong turn, it was soon clear that the driver needed to hustle along and, if possible, build up a cushion of time. The kicker, however, was that you never knew when the segment would end. You could come around a corner and be surprised to see the timer waiting for you. If you'd been averaging a faster time than specified your only hope was that there was space for you to stop prior to the check point where you could sit to let the clock tick down to your appointed time. Given that our only mathematical tool, at that time, was the aforementioned slide rule, Wayne quickly found himself to be extremely busy!

However, in this first rally, an event that we desperately wanted to win, all of this soon became academic. We'd gone only a few miles when the right front of the car started to vigorously thump and bounce. We'd blown a tire- So much for us trying to keep to a schedule. I pulled the car off to the side of the road, and we proceeded to do our best imitation of a NASCAR pit crew changing tires. Of course, with a scissor jack, and a L-handle lug wrench, it took us somewhat longer to put on our "new" rubber.

I have emphasized above the word new. The tires on the car were old-probably the tires that had originally come on the car when it had been delivered nine years previously. While the tires still had plenty of tread on them, they were nearly rotten. And, the spare, unfortunately, was in the same, or worse, condition. But, that thought, of course, never crossed our minds. All we could think of was getting the tire changed, and getting back into the rally. And, in less than five minutes we were again under way- desperate to make up the lost time. Of course, it was, despite my inspired fast driving, not possible to completely recover that deficit. Consequently, we didn't win that rally. But, we had learned a lot about what you needed to do to win.

The most important thing that we discovered, apart from the need for new tires, was that a slide rule, despite Wayne's desperate attempts to calculate our average speed, was not really practical. We needed something else if we were to succeed. Fortunately, another perusal of the automotive book store's ads showed that we could order a set of tables that contained pre-calculated required segment times given any combination of covered miles and specified average speeds. Now, with that, we knew that we were in business. We couldn't wait for the next event to put this new tool to use. Fortunately, we didn't have to wait long.

The next rally, two months later, took place at the Mercedes Benz dealership in Winter Haven. After we registered we took a few minutes to look over our competition. We were most worried about the couple entered in a new XKE Jaguar roadster. I knew from having observed a couple of recent gymkhanas that the driver was the Club's champion and president. Obviously, he had to be taken seriously. Another entrant was in a new Porsche 911. There were also a couple of Corvettes entered, as well as multiple MGs, Triumphs, and other more common sports cars. In fact, every car entered was a much, much more capable machine than my lowly, underpowered, very used Dauphine. But, we had rally tables- and, as far as we could see, no one else did.

We left the starting line feeling confident. But, that confidence was soon put to the test when we made a wrong turn. In no more than a few miles we were already badly off schedule. Fortunately, we were soon able to get back on the correct course, and, using our new tables, we were able to easily see how much time we had to make up. Some inspired driving, and careful navigating, allowed us to get back on schedule. Long story short- despite the high dollar sports cars that we were competing against, we won the rally. First place for a couple of high school seniors competing against experienced adults in much more expensive cars! We were over the moon!

Two months later there was another rally on the schedule. But, by now Wayne had gotten his own car and, of course, he also wanted to drive. So, I agreed to take on the navigation role- assured by our new tables that no high level math, or slide rule calculations, would be required. We won that rally, too. Although, if my memory serves me correctly, we didn't find out that we'd actually won until several days after the event. The rally's organizer had incorrectly calculated the results. A phone call notified us of the mistake, and we eventually received the improperly presented trophy. But, if I remember, after two wins in a row we were beginning to feel slightly less welcome by the club's membership.

It seems like we may have run, and won, another event in my car. But, I can't be sure about that. In any case, we soon had graduated from school. That, and other events, and then leaving for college, kept us from being able to enter any additional rallies. But, the aged Renault had done itself proud- it had proven to be the very capable rally car, with excellent road holding and sufficient speed, that I had always known it would be. And, its driver, I reasoned, had done well, too.

The Lucas Flamethrower:

Each year in the early 1960s the automotive magazines would extensively cover the Monte Carlo Rally. This unique event featured cars, in the dead of the European winter, starting from widely divergent locations (London, Paris, Berlin, Brussels, Vienna, Moscow, etc.), following specified routes as they drove rapidly, day and night, across the continent with the ultimate goal of converging for a final special Alpine rally stage before driving to the finish in Monte Carlo. This important event had been envisioned by Albert I, Prince of Monaco- what better way to attract wealthy tourists to Monaco from the capital cities of Europe in the middle of winter? It had been first run in 1911.

Following World War II the event had become one of the world's major automotive events, and from the 1960's onwards pure speed had played an increasingly important role in the results. During this time, automotive manufacturers were looking at this rally as an important opportunity to highlight the speed and reliability of their latest vehicles. Rally's had become cool!

And, one of the coolest aspects of the cars then competing were the banks of huge driving lights that some of the cars fitted to the fronts of the vehicles to enable the drivers to see better as they sped through the night.   I should probably mention again, before going further, that a Renault Dauphine had distinguished itself by winning this event outright in 1958. And, mounted prominently in the center, on top, of the front bumper of that winning car was a large driving, or fog, light. Given my involvement in the local rally scene, and given my commitment to all things related to Renault Dauphine, I had to have a light like this.

My research through the magazine pages led me to the "Lucas Flamethrower" driving light. Who could resist a name like that? If I remember correctly, it produced 1 million candle power of light- probably close to ten times the amount of light produced by the car's standard lights. Whoa!!!!!!

The light soon arrived in the mail, and was quickly installed and wired with a dash mounted on/off switch by a local garage. The light was mounted on the bumper in the exactly the same location as the Monte Carlo winner. It looked good! And, the light it produced was nothing short of amazing- it was almost better than daylight! I loved that light.

Run-Ins with the Law:

It was inevitable, of course, given my enthusiasm for driving the Dauphine quickly that I would eventually come to the attention of the authorities. I'll share two such adventures.

The first took place after on a quiet Saturday evening. As I remember, my younger sister and I had driven to the nearby town of Ft. Meade to visit with our aunt- Audrey Davis. We spent the evening with her, having dinner, and watching television. A little after eleven thirty we left for home, arriving on the deserted dark streets of our home as the witching hour struck. Given that no one else was on the highway I was perhaps proceeding with some "enthusiasm," but not, in my opinion, dangerously so. However, I do believe that I may have exited the divided main road and turned into my neighborhood street with my usual fervor, demonstrating the proper maximum corner radius and tight apex techniques that I had so carefully studied. The same when I made the right hander into the street in front of my family's house. It wasn't until I was stopped in the front yard, and we were just beginning to exit the car, that the police cruiser, lights and siren announcing its presence, slid to a stop behind me. Then, the officer, with the assistance of his car's loud speaker, instructed me loudly to remain in the car. All of this commotion, of course, had stirred my parents, who soon sleepily emerged from the house, hands shielding their eyes from the glare, to see what the heck was going on. Given the presence of my irritated father, and the absence of any type of illegal beverages, the cop quickly decided that the only action required would be for him to deliver a stern warning about not driving so fast in the future. I seem to remember him saying as he left, in an aside to my father, that he didn't think that a car with as little horsepower as my Renault was capable of going as fast as it had been going. Rather than being insulted, I took that as a compliment!

The second episode was rather more embarrassing, and was something that I regret doing to this day- chiefly because it was so stupid! Again- a quiet evening in Mulberry- I think it was maybe a weekend night. Regardless, there was nothing going on. I was driving the Renault when I crossed paths with some friends in a Volkswagen Beetle. I think a guy that I knew was driving, and there were a couple of girls with him. Somehow, the encounter evolved into an impromptu road race- Beetle in front, and my Dauphine right on his bumper. Then, for some reason, at the last minute the driver in front decided to make a right-handed turn onto a side street that ran through a neighborhood of newly built homes. His decision had been made so late that he couldn't slow sufficiently, slid wide, and came to a near stop. Seeing my opportunity, I executed a perfectly controlled inside pass, leaving the other car behind. But, then, as soon I stop looking in the mirror to admire my handiwork, what I saw caused me to slam on the brakes and come to a screeching halt. Standing in the middle of the road- his arms outstretched- was a large man in civilian clothes. But, not just any man- the guy standing in the road blocking my way was the town's off-duty, Chief of Police! I figured that, without question, I was going to jail. But, for some unknown reason, he didn't call for backup. Rather he only delivered an angry, expletive laden, adult-oriented lecture- and then, miraculously, let me go. I, in oh so many ways, was lucky!

Chapter Eight: Fate

I graduated from high school in 1966- a young man ready to take on the world. I had been accepted by, and had enrolled in, Stetson University in Deland, Florida. This excellent, small school- The "Harvard of the South"- had appealed to me for two reasons: first, my father had graduated from this school; and second, and perhaps more importantly, Deland is located only a few miles away from Daytona International Speedway! It seemed to all make sense to me. Where better to go to school?

But, before I could begin my studies fate intruded in a very dramatic fashion. One summer day my family decided to take our boat to Scott Lake for an afternoon of water skiing. We invited a number of our friends to join us. I was riding with my friend Jimmy Sweat in his brand new Plymouth Barracuda. Two other guys were in the back seat. I remember that we had spent several hours boating and skiing, before rain and wind intervened and forced an end to the outing. We helped Dad load the boat, and then headed home. We intentionally pulled out ahead of Dad- since we knew that he would be driving slowly pulling the boat. But, he normally drove like that anyway. We were driving south on Highway 37, a two lane road. We were taking it easy since the roads were slick from the recent rain. I remember that we were listening on the radio to, and happily singing along with, the Beatles "Yellow Submarine." We were just four young men, none with a care in the world.

The traffic heading north was heavy, but moving fast. But, we weren't surprised, knowing that the mines would have just changed shifts and, as was customary, all those first shift workers would be in a hurry to get home, or to get to the bar. We were approaching a cross road at what is now Carter Road when we could see the north bound traffic begin to slow as an oncoming car had stopped to turn left. But, just as we came alongside that stopped car we were shocked to see a fast moving northbound car lockup its tires as its surprised driver tried to brake for the stopped cars in front. As this happened, that car- a big, heavy, older Oldsmobile- slid directly into our path. It was probably still moving about sixty miles per hour- our speed was likely only slightly less. The collision was huge.

Jimmy and I were both wearing the car's seat belts. At that time there were only lap belts- no shoulder straps. The two guys in the back were not buckled in- I don't believe that rear seat belts were even available back then.

I didn't wake up for several days. When the cars collided my body had pivoted forward around the lap belt, and my face had planted itself into the poorly padded dashboard. Jimmy's face had hit the steering wheel. We were both in bad shape. The two guys in the back seemed, at the time, to have gotten away with only minor injuries. I heard much later, however, that one of them had suffered back injuries in the crash that troubled him for the rest of his life.

My parents, my sister, and her friends, arrived at the scene of the crash shortly after it occurred. No one ever spoke much to me about how they reacted- but, I can imagine what it must have been like.

Jimmy and I, according to what we were later told, were loaded into the same ambulance for the trip to Lakeland's hospital. At that time, we were unconscious, and our conditions were both serious. From what I've been told, during the trip I never woke up. Jimmy, however, would wake up occasionally, see me lying beside him in a bloody heap, and kindly try to use a towel to wipe the blood from my face. However, as soon as he did that, he'd collapse into unconsciousness again, leaving the towel covering my face, greatly complicating my efforts to breathe.

As it turned out, Jimmy and I were fortunate to have survived. We both suffered severe facial and head injuries. I lost all my upper front teeth, and required extensive plastic surgery. And, although it was never discussed at that time, I knew that I had also suffered a very severe concussion. As months and years passed, I could tell that my mental faculties had been significantly impaired. I just wasn't as 'sharp' as I had been before the accident. I couldn't read as well, I couldn't think as well, I couldn't do math as well, and most importantly to me, I couldn't drive as well, either. My reactions just weren't what they had been. Prior to that accident there had been no doubt in my mind that I had what it took to succeed in racing. Afterwards, I knew that I no longer possessed the same capabilities. As the decades went past I think that I recovered most of what I had lost- but, I doubt I was ever again quite as good as I had once been.

The facial injuries, surgery, and dental damage didn't do much for the impression I made a month or so later when I arrived on my college campus. Definitely, no girl friends my freshman year!

Chapter Nine: Taruffi's Fifth Requirement

The next four years were spent in undergraduate school, followed, nine months later, by two years in the US Army. These were the years of the Viet Nam war, and the 'draft.' Initially, you could defer being drafted into the service simply by being enrolled in college, but it was understood that as soon as you graduated you would then be drafted. One alternative to this scenario was to enroll in the Reserve Officers Training Corp while in school. This committed you to a two year period of military service after graduation, but allowed you to then enter the service as an officer rather than the alternative of being drafted in as a buck private. I chose ROTC. From my perspective this strategy worked well since I was able to avoid serving in Viet Nam. Several of my friends never came back from there.

I did OK in school, but I certainly didn't distinguish myself. The highlights of my time there, in order of importance, were the Sebring 12 Hour, the Daytona 24 Hour, the US Grand Prix, girl friends, surfing, and obtaining my Psychology degree.

During my junior year I got to know a fellow in my dorm who was also inflicted with the racing bug- he was eaten up with it at least as badly as me. Fred Lewis was his name, and subsequently, we traveled together to races many, many times. He was a good friend. I remember that he was much more astute technically, and mechanically, than I was, while all that I really cared about was the driving!

Fred and I spend a lot of good times together traveling to various races. Two of the highlights were the trips we made, in 1969 and 1970, to the US Grand Prix in Watkins Glen, New York. The first of these races was won by Jochen Rindt, but what I remember most was the inspired drive to second place by Piers Courage. He put on a fantastic display of bravery and car control. Unfortunately, both of these drivers would soon perish while at the wheels of their F1 cars.

The 1970 race was distinguished by it being Emerson Fittipaldi's first F1 victory- driving for Team Lotus following Jochen Rindt's death. I recall that he won after putting in a rather careful drive. Jackie Steward had dominated most of the race before his engine seized up. Jackie Ickx, driving for Ferrari had been in second until his car experienced a problem. My first driving hero, Pedro Rodriquez then ran in the lead- with much support from me- before running short of fuel. Eventually, he would finish second. The surprise win of Fittipaldi was almost shocking. After all it was his first victory, in only his fourth grand prix. This dashing, handsome young man seemed to be on top of the world. I remember feeling slightly aggrieved as we made the long drive back to Florida- Emerson Fittapaldi, the same age as me, was sitting exactly where I had always hoped that I would. It didn't help that we had also seen in the local newspaper a picture of his beautiful, happy Brazilian wife. In contrast, at that time, all I had was an appointment with the US Army to learn how to shoot cannons.

It dawn on me during this drive home that Taruffi's fifth requirement for a successful racing career- "A Good Bank Balance"- was actually a very serious impediment to my future racing career. I had no money, and no prospect of acquiring any soon. Much to my dismay, no one had, as of yet, come forward with an offer to pay me to drive their racing car. In fact, the only way that I could now envision ever having enough money to go racing was to figure out some way to earn it. For the next twenty years I set about trying to make that happen.

Chapter Ten: Skippy School- The Dream Comes True

After two years in the Army; three years in graduate school; and fourteen years into a banking career, I had finally earned enough money to blow some of it on racing. This was not the easiest decision to make-and, certainly not the smartest. After all I was then married, with a mortgage and car payments, and two kids that would eventually need to go to college. But, time was passing. Does the term 'mid-life crisis' mean anything to you? I was forty years old- if ever I was going to begin racing, I had to do it then. I sent away a letter asking for information on "The Skip Barber Racing School."

Skip Barber had been a moderately successful U.S. racing driver back when I was attending college. Once the drives ran out he recognized, and acted on satisfying, the need for a racing school for aspiring drivers in the U.S. Over time his school, and the techniques that it taught, had been very successful. In fact, the school had begun to brag in its advertisements that most of the country's successful pro-drivers had attended the Barber School. And, critically, I knew that the school had recently begun offering its racing school program at Sebring International Raceway! How could I say no?

The core program for the Skip Barber School was a three-day racing school that combined classroom instruction with equal time in a Formula Ford racing car. It was billed as every driver's gateway to motorsports and racing! Sounded exactly like what I was looking for.

Registration for the school took place at the Sebring Holiday Inn. I was amazed at the number of guys waiting in line to sign-up for the school. There had to have been forty, or more. Once the paperwork was out of the way, everyone gathered for the pre-school briefing. Other than the time we were to be at the track (early!), the most important information was the warning to the students about not driving to and from the track in their driving suits, and, by all means, not driving too fast through town. It seems that the local cops absolutely loved to stop racing school students.

The next morning the students were assigned to one of two groups. The first group went to do an exercise in the race cars; the second went to a classroom lecture. I remember being disappointed that I was in the second group. But, it really didn't matter since the groups would rotate every two hours, or so.

The classroom session got right to the good stuff by discussing the proper racing line (Taruffi smiled!), downshifting a standard transmission (not a problem for me!), threshold braking (a new term, and technique), and proper cornering techniques (now we're talking!) There was just enough stuff that I didn't already know to make me think that I wasn't wasting my money. So far, so good! As we were sitting in class we could eventually begin to hear tires squealing, and engines roaring, as the first group worked on their in-car exercises. I couldn't wait to take my turn in the car!

A couple of hours later the classroom session adjourned, and the two instruction groups swapped places. At first, the in-car session was boring, and basic. How to start it? How to read a tachometer? How to use a clutch and how to shift gears? Come on guys- I've been doing this stuff since I was a kid. But, eventually, we got to drive the cars. Granted, it was just maneuvering around cones in the paddock- but, still- I was actually driving a real race car. The highlight of the session was a discussion of "TTO," or, trailing throttle over-steer. In other words, if you pop off of the throttle while you are cornering, weight will transfer from the rear wheels to the front, and you will immediately spin. The instructor asked for volunteers to demonstrate this concept, and, of course, I immediately raised my hand. I was confident that if there was one thing that I could do, I could spin the car. And, I did- just the way the instructor said to do it. I was proud. I couldn't believe that many of the other students were actually frightened at the thought of spinning a car. But, eventually, everyone got the hang of it. From that it was on to exercises that involved driving the proper racing line, threshold braking, downshifting, and cornering techniques. Actually, doing the stuff that we'd just talked about in class! At that point I was glad that we'd done the classroom stuff first.

After lunch, it was back to the classroom for more instruction while the first group was back to driving the cars. Finally, it was our turn to drive again. This time we practiced a downshifting exercise which actually had us driving as fast as we could up the pit straight before braking and downshifting in preparation for turning 180 degrees into the pit lane (did anyone say "hairpin corner?"), and roaring down it as fast as we could go before making another hairpin, and repeating the exercise. This went on for almost thirty minutes, as the instructors closely observed what we were doing. If our techniques weren't correct we got waived into the 'pits' by the instructor who calmly critiqued us and suggested improvements. If I remember correctly I only got waived in one time- and that was because they'd noticed that I'd begun to skip all the double clutching stuff since I'd discovered that the racing transmission would easily slip into a lower gear as you just blipped the throttle. My hero Phil Hill had written about doing just that in one of the magazine articles that I'd read as a kid. The instructor, if I remember, was impressed, but suggested that I should stay with the program. The other thing that I remember about this exercise was that I was faster around these laps than many of the others.

Later we got to drive the cars around the track! Granted, we had to follow the instructor's street car around the track, single file. But, still- I was actually driving a racing car around a race track! Yeah!

The day had flown by. It seemed like no time before we were back at the hotel. The first place I headed was into the swimming pool. I couldn't believe how hot and tired I was. Who knew that driving a car could be so physically tiring?

Eventually, the pool filled with other students who also needed to cool off. After a while, and a few beers, we began to talk with each other. I remember that we talked about the school and asked each other how they'd done during the day. Basically, as men will do, we were sizing each other up. One guy (Dave Devaney), I learned, was even doing the school for the second time- going through it with his brother. I was actually glad to hear that this was his second time through the class since he had looked like he knew what he was doing, and had been quick. This guy eventually complimented me on my driving- noting that it had looked like I knew what I was doing, too. He asked if I'd raced before? I assured him that I hadn't, but that I'd spent my whole life studying how to do it. I was pleased that he'd noticed my skills.

The second day was more of the same: Classroom instruction and on track exercises; Theory, and application: followed by more theory, and more application. Repetition was the order of the day, with immediate feedback from the instructors, and then back onto the track to do it again. More braking exercises, and then the day concluded with a competition flag talk. This had been a very full day- designed to help the participant transition from student to racer. I remember being so exhausted when I got back to the hotel that all I wanted to do was shower, get something to eat, and go to bed! The next morning came early. As I got up I noticed that I was stiff, and covered with bruises from battering about inside the car. This racing stuff was more physical than I had imagined.

The third day of the school incorporated race craft, as we tried to apply the things that we'd learned. We practiced racing starts, and racing restarts. Then, we completed several passing, and drafting exercises. The second half of the day was dedicated to open lapping- driving a race car as fast as I could around an actual race track. Of course, every lap was observed, and timed. As the saying goes, "When the green flag drops, the bull shit stops!" Every lap that we made was timed. When I reviewed the timing sheets I discovered that while I could drive, I certainly wasn't the fastest driver at the school. I was pleased to see that I had been quicker than many, but disappointed that I wasn't near the top of the results. But, I quickly reasoned that since some of the guys were going through the school for the second time, that since a few of the guys actually had prior racing experience, and, that since many of the guys were much, much younger, I shouldn't be too discouraged. I concluded that I was good, but not yet great. I needed more practice- I needed seat time.

In conclusion, the Skip Barber Racing School Three Day Program was excellent. I loved it, and I have recommended it highly ever since.

A few months later, after letting the school experience sink in, I began to feel the strong need to drive a race car again. Fortunately, the good folks at Skip Barber had anticipated this, and had other programs in their curriculum designed to satisfy this need- Lapping days, and Racing series. All that was required was to have competed the school (or have other suitable experience), and to have the required funds. Fortunately, at that time, I satisfied both of those requirements. We loaded the family up for our first racing weekend.

This experience was a giant step up from the school. There were guys doing this stuff that had done it for years- guys doing it who were very experienced, and very fast! When qualifying for the race was completed I was faster than some, but closer to the back than to the front of the field. I needed to go about two seconds faster.

In practice, I tried pushing harder. That helped some, but not enough. It also caused me to spin on a couple of occasions- once rather wildly as I pushed hard through a high-speed bend. During the next day's race I didn't finish last, but I do remember actually being lapped by the leaders on the last lap of the race. I tried, as we entered the track's fast Turn One to not get in their way, but….. as instructed, I held my line. The leader got by successfully- the second place guy got held up slightly.

Bottom line- I'd learned that I could race. I wasn't yet fast, but I could drive- okay. Clearly I needed more practice- I needed more seat time. I reckoned that I could get that eventually. So, in the way that foolish, mid-life-crisis afflicted males will do, I concluded that logically I needed to move on to bigger, better, faster, and more expensive things?

Chapter Eleven: Going Pro!

My experience with Skip Barber had been positive. I'd learned a lot. As far as I was concerned, the program had been a success. But, spending a lot of money to continue to drive Formula Fords was not exactly what I wanted to do.

At that time (1990), the nation's largest sports car racing series was conducted by the International Motor Sports Association (IMSA). This organization sanctioned most of the major sports car races in the country- including, critically for me, the Sebring Twelve Hour. I understood well that I wasn't ready, either from an experience standpoint or financially, to be able to aspire to doing that race. But, I knew that there was a support race prior to the Twelve Hour- a race that I would be eligible to enter. To make that happen, all I would need to do would be to get my IMSA license, and then find a ride! As it turned out neither of those requirements proved to be a problem.

A friend of mine, knew a guy in Miami, who knew a guy, who knew another guy that was putting together a team for the race that I was interested in entering- the Sebring 4-hour Firestone Firehawk Endurance Race. This race was perfect for me- long enough for me to gain valuable seat time; an extremely competitive field; it was part of a gateway professional series; and, most importantly, it was going to be held at the Sebring International Raceway. I called the guy that my friend had mentioned. As it turned out he had already rented out his available seat. But, he knew another guy who was building a car. So, I called that guy. He had a seat! A tentative deal was quickly agreed.

The fellow that I had spoken to was Mike Scharnow. He, and his brother, Mark, had plans to race a Dodge Shelby Charger in the Sports

Division of the Firehawk series. On paper, the car sounded fast. I made plans to meet them, and take a look at the car, at the Miami Grand Prix, a month before the Sebring race. My family and I weren't able to come down early to see them race, but we did get to see the car, and meet the guys. The car and the equipment looked good, and Mike and Mark seemed like standup guys. We shook hands on the deal.

The agreement was that Mike, Mark and I would all drive in the 4 hour race. For some reason, the fact that I had never driven a front-wheel drive race car, or had never raced in a professional series didn't seem to concern either them, or me, all that much. I guess they needed my money, and I, of course, was simply ready to go racing. I was stoked.

Unfortunately, our preparation at the track didn't go well. For some, at that time, unknown reason the engine wouldn't run without misfiring- badly. There was something obviously wrong with the electrical system. The guys threw everything they could think of at the car. But, nothing seemed to help. We missed all of the first practice session. Finally, in the last practice session before the race the brothers decided that I had to get in the car to at least gain some familiarity and experience with the track and the car. But, the engine still wasn't running right. On the track, I, essentially, could do nothing other than trundle around slowly for a few laps, trying to stay out of the way, before the session mercifully ended.

All afternoon, and all night, the brothers and their crew continued to work on the car. But, nothing helped. It still wouldn't run. Finally, only minutes before the race was scheduled to begin, their father arrived, having driven up from Miami with a different set of spark plug wires to replace the brand new, highly priced set that the brothers had installed when preparing the car. That simple step, almost miraculously, was the answer to the problem. Now, the engine was running fine.

Since we had missed qualifying we had to start dead last in the field. Mark drove the car in the opening session. He immediately began to pass cars, moving up rapidly. He drove until the car needed to be refueled- he was in the car for about an hour. Now it was my turn. Mark hopped out; and the crew stuffed me in the car, and strapped me tight! Ready or not, I was about to make my debut in a big time professional motor race. I was hardly well prepared. But, now, it was time to see what I was made of.

The first few laps were definitely exploratory. I had to find my braking points; locate turn in points; and determine how to clip the apexes. But, soon it began to feel quite natural. I began to have fun.

After all this time I only have a few memories of my time in the car. Part way through my stint I remember catching a car- a Ford- and racing closely with it for several laps, before finally passing it. It was actually the first time in my racing career that I'd been able to race for an extended period with another car. I had enjoyed it! After the race, I looked up the driver of that car in the paddock, and introduced myself. He was a guy a little older than me by the name of Dick Ruhl. Nice guy, who owned a Ford dealership in Ohio. Over the years we became friends.

Another memory was that there was an extended full-course caution in place during my stint. Driving at pace car speed, following in a line of cars, the heat inside the car was extreme. At one point I squeezed my left hand out the open window besides the window safety net in an attempt to scoop in some cooler air. After the race I learned that my sister, who had come to the track to observe my race, had seen me do this. She actually thought that I was waving at her. Of course, I had no idea where she was watching the race from.

The final memory of my time in the car was of the noise that the engine made. The tail pipe exited the left side of the car, in front of the rear tire. Normally, driving down the straight, the noise was not remarkable. But, when going through Turn One, a very fast left hand bend with a tall concrete wall next to the turn's apex, was a different experience. The exhaust sound ricocheted against the wall and back into the driver's window. I thought that was cool.

Eventually, I received a signal from the pits that it was time to come in. I acknowledged the pit board, and came in the next lap to turn the car over to Mike. The car was refueled, and he roared back into the race.

When I checked the standings I saw that I had done okay. I hadn't passed many people, but I hadn't been passed either. And, I hadn't crashed out, or damaged the car. I thought that I had done okay for a first time driver.

Mike, a very experienced driver, immediately picked up the pace and began to pass cars. As time went by we were just beginning to think about actually achieving a decent finish when Mike failed to come around. As it turned out, the car's engine had stopped just as he had come onto the back straight. Some critical component had broken. We were out.

After the race, after we'd commiserated, and after we'd packed up, Mike and I compared notes. Bottom line- I was pleased with the team; and he was pleased with my performance. We agreed to stay in touch.

A few weeks later we talked again, and I agreed to join the team again for an upcoming race at West Palm Beach.

Long story short- this time the car ran well. However, during my practice session the car ran out of fuel- leaving me stranded on course. But, at least we got a good idea on how many laps we could run before we needed to refuel. I started the race, and drove my stint without issues. I remember passing a number of cars and having a good time. I really didn't want to have to come in to turn the car over to Mike. Things were looking good for us. Unfortunately, almost as soon as Mike took over the skies darkened, and shortly thereafter began to steadily drizzle.

A few laps later, with the track now having become very greasy, Mike crashed the car- hard. The track's last turn was a 180 degree horseshoe shaped corner that led onto the front straight. He, trying too hard, locked up the car's tires under braking, and slid headfirst into the outside wall. It took quite some time before Mike was extricated from the car. Then he was transported to the on-site medical unit for care and evaluation. Evidently, his helmet had impacted one of the roll bars in the car. When he finally got back to the pits the only wound we could see was a cut to his nose. But, I suspect he may have also sustained a mild concussion. He certainly didn't seem quite himself. And, again, we were out of a race. Later it was determined that the impact had totaled the car. Eventually, it had to be sold for scrap.

Mike and I met the next day and discussed where we might go from there. Clearly we were out of business for the coming season, but possibly, we concluded, we might look to putting together a program for the following season. Given the previous day's accident, Mike may not have thinking all that clearly. As for me, well- once the racing bug bites....

Chapter Twelve: Caribbean Motor Sports

A couple of weeks later Mike called to report some interesting news. He'd talked with a guy and had learned that Honda had a program for teams that raced their cars in the Firestone Firehawk Series. From our standpoint, it sounded almost too good to be true. If you finished a race in one of the top three positions, Honda would match the prize money that you'd earned. In addition, Honda would provide free parts to those racing their cars. They also provided race engineering support, and a parts trailer, at the actual races. It was also rumored that Honda would even provide free cars to some teams! We were sold. We would definitely be racing Hondas. Now, all we needed were some actual cars, and a trailer.

In the fall of the year we made the decision to purchase a couple of Honda CRXs. We had determined that the rumored availability of free cars from the factory had not exactly been factual. It was, in fact, true that Honda would sometimes provide free cars, but they would only provide those to established, and successful, race teams- something we definitely were not. We would first need to purchase cars, and then race them successfully to prove that we were worthy of additional consideration. But, while disappointing, that only seemed fair.

As a result of these conversations with Honda's racing chief we learned that one of the top Honda teams in the Touring Division of the Series- the class in which we wanted to run- was selling one of its cars. I contacted the team's owner, T.C. Kline, and we quickly made a deal. T.C. and I agreed that we could pick the car up after the season's last race in Watkins Glen, New York. I would need to bring a cashier's check. Now, we needed a trailer.

Mike and I had decided that we should look to run a two car team. While I didn't actually have the money to fund a second car, we were hopeful that we might find someone who did. Someone who could help us fund the entire operation. For racers- hope certainly springs eternal. We agreed that the new team would be named Caribbean Motor Sports- in honor of our Miami base of operations.

Shortly thereafter I placed an order for a two car trailer- it would be built at a factory in Ohio, which, coincidently, was located near an Interstate Highway upon which we could travel to get to Watkins Glen. Road Trip!

Mike, and his wife, Karen, owned a Chevrolet Suburban, a vehicle capable (we thought) to pull the trailer. We quickly put together what seemed at the time like a "reasonable" plan to drive to Ohio, pick up the trailer, and then pull the trailer to New York to load the car, and then drive the rig back to Florida- all over the course of a weekend! Mike, his brother Mark, and two of their friends (and race team members) John Schunzel, and John Petit, agreed to make the trip with me. Five of us in a Suburban- driving non-stop from Florida, to Ohio, then on to New York, and, finally, back to Florida! Does that sound like fun to you? Racers have sometimes been rumored to be just a little bit crazy!

The first part of the trip went smoothly- no issues. We quickly developed a driving rotation. The driver, and the driver that would succeed him, rode in the front; two passengers rested in the back seat; while the just relieved driver stretched out and slept in the large luggage area of the SUV. We stopped only for gas and food. The one exception was when we drove through Indianapolis. After all, we were a bunch of racers. A quick calculation confirmed that we had time to visit the Indianapolis Motor Speedway! I remember all of us riding in the tour bus that circled the track. The highlight of that tour was when we each got to drive that bus for a short distance on the track. At least we could all then truthfully claim that we had driven at Indy!

Two hours later we were back on the road- heading north to Ohio. Later we pulled up at the trailer factory, signed the necessary paperwork, wrote the required check, and hooked the rig onto the Suburban. An hour later, we were driving towards New York- a shiny new race trailer proudly towing behind the Suburban.

The drive from Ohio to New York was fairly lengthy- we drove through the night. The next morning, somewhere in the woods of western New York we groggily stopped for gasoline, food, and coffee. I purchased a local newspaper, curious if there might be any news about the race at Watkins Glen (remember this was pre-internet). Surprisingly, we did find a short story concerning the previous day's events at the track. One paragraph in the article described how a driver, identified as Mitch Payton, had flipped his car on the track. Payton, the story related, was a paraplegic. But, fortunately, the driver had been rescued unharmed by the track's safety crew. We thought that was a pretty cool story, and drove happily to the track- intent on our mission of picking up our new race car. Later we pulled into the paddock at Watkins Glen, and began to search for T.C. Kline's compound. It was not hard to find- parked right in front were the dented, mangled remains of a car that had, all too obviously, been rolled. The car that we had read about in the paper was the car that I was supposed to buy! Crap! Now what?

I quickly found T.C., and explored the options. Could I buy his other car instead? After all, I had a cashier's check already made out to him. No. He explained that other car belonged to Honda, and could not be sold. That option was, therefore, out of the question. At that time I wondered if that reluctance to sell was because of some special modifications that Honda had built into that car: tricks that they didn't want anyone else to know about or have access to. Later, however, I learned that the legal team at Honda had put restrictions on how the cars that they provided a team could be disposed of.

In desperation, I approached the owner of the team that was T.C. Kline's primary competitor, Sandy Santullo. He owned, and drove for, a team called Copper Kettle Racing. I later learned that his team was named after a marina that his family owned on one of the great lakes. This team, with the assistance of a driver by the name of Lance Stewart, had actually won that season's championship. Therefore, I figured the cars should be at least as good as Kline's. But, it was a good news- bad news story. Santullo agreed to sell me his championship winning car. But, he wouldn't accept my personal check- remember I had a cashier's check made out to T.C. Kline. End of the day, I agreed to buy the car, and he agreed to get it to Florida once my check had cleared.

Now there was nothing left to do but load everyone back in the Suburban, and drag an empty trailer back to Florida. Talk about feeling deflated! And, worried. All we could think about now was whether the Copper Kettle team was going to ship us the car as it had been raced, or whether they were going, after they got it back to the garage, to strip off the good stuff from it. Fortunately, when the car was delivered to Miami a few weeks later it appeared to be just as we had last seen it.

In the meantime, we had been talking with a young racer named Cass Whitehead. Cass was from Atlanta, and worked at Road Atlanta as a racing instructor. He was a quick driver. He had learned, possibly through Honda, what we were doing, and potentially wanted to race with us. Eventually, we agreed that if he would buy a second car, we would run it for him. Any money earned from that car, either from prizes or from renting out the second seat, would come to us. With that, we were ready to go racing.

Cass set about looking for a car. As it turned out the only good car then available was the car that we had tried to buy initially. T.C. Kline had rebuilt it, and claimed that it was as good as ever. Almost unbelievably, the rolled car that we'd had to leave in Watkins Glen eventually came to race with us after all.

Chapter Thirteen: Caribbean Motor Sports' First Season

The team's first race would be in February of the next year. But, we couldn't wait that long to drive our new car- we wanted to "test" it. I mean you couldn't just show up for a race with a car that you'd never driven? Towards that end, Mike rented the old Hialeah Speedway for a day. The course on which we would run consisted of the drag strip, and parallel return road, connected by short strips of pavement on either end. Pretty basic- but, it was available at the right price. The only frill being the ambulance and accompanying medics that the track required with the rental.

Given that the track was in South Florida it had, of course, rained the morning of the test. By the time we were ready to get started the track had begun to dry though it still had substantial puddles in some spots. But, that couldn't be helped. We wanted to drive the car.

I remember that Mike took the car out first. I then got in it. And, Mark had the next session. There were no issues, and the laps had gotten progressively faster as the track had dried. Eventually, it was my turn, again. By now the puddles and moisture were gone. It was time to go fast! And, I was determined to not be the slowest of the drivers. Consequently, I was hard on the power, and the car felt great. I did probably a dozen laps- it was hard to stop- I was having too much fun. Eventually, I decided I should only do one more lap, and then bring it in to the pits. But, I wanted that last lap to be fast- hopefully, the quickest of the day! Consequently, I was pushing harder than I'd pushed before. Coming into the final corner I was flying. All I had left to do was nail the final 180 degree turn. To make sure that I didn't leave any time on the track, I left my braking for the corner just a little later than I had done before. Oh, shoot! I locked up the front tires, and before I could do anything the car slid hard into the tire wall. The guys told me later that they were convinced that the car was going to roll. This was certainly not a good way to impress my new team mates!

Given this exhibition of driving talent I concluded that I could benefit from additional Skip Barber Racing School instruction. Specifically, I was attracted to a course labeled a "Car Control Clinic." It sounded like exactly what I needed.

A few weeks later I was back in Sebring- this time sitting in a small office in the school's garage with just one other student, and the instructor. The instructor was none other than Terry Earwood- Skip Barber's Chief Instructor.

We sat in the office for a short time as Terry went over some key handling concepts. Then we drove out to the track's skid pad- each student wheeling one of the schools' uniquely modified 5-series BMWs. The skid pad was wet- with a large oscillating sprinkler set in the middle of the turn on each end ensuring that the pavement would never dry out. Now, it was our job to apply the principles of car control that Terry had just lectured us on- working towards not only being able to quickly and reliably lap the figure eight track, but more importantly, being able to recover from lurid slides and skids. Terry would ride in the cars' passenger side front seat- passing along instructions and suggestions- but also, sometimes pulling on a hidden lever to create slides that we had to deal with. Sometimes, he would even push down on my throttle leg, making sure that I used all of the power available. I've never, before or since, had so much fun.

After lunch we returned to the lecture room, before switching back to driving. But, now, rather than sliding the school's BMW's on a skid pad, we were tasked with driving Formula Ford race cars around a mini-road course. The goal was to apply all the lessons that we'd learned from sliding around in the wet to these open wheel race cars circulating on a dry race track. And, of course, this time all of our laps would be timed.

The day ended all too soon. I'd learned a great deal, and had had more fun than I'd ever thought possible. It had been money well spent.

In the meantime, Mike and Mark (and the other guys, too) had been hard at work. Both cars had been painted in our team colors- day glow orange and Caribbean blue. They looked resplendent. The guys had also outfitted, and modified, the team's new trailer- to ensure that it was ready to support us at the track. I was particularly impressed with the hidden storage lockers that they had built into the floor. The cars, of course, had also received their close attention. We were ready for the track.

The Team's first race was a four hour enduro that served as a preliminary event to the Sebring 12 Hour- the same race that we had run together the previous year. But, this year, as opposed to the previous year's chaos trying to get the car to even run, we were well prepared and organized.

Cass, for his part, had talked a quick young driving instructor into paying to join him in his car; and I had convinced Dave Devaney (see Sebring Skip Barber School) to join me in mine. For, this race Mike and Mark were going to crew, along with the same guys who had joined us on the trip to Watkins Glen. Bill Wilkins, a friend and neighbor from my home in Clermont, Florida was also part of the team.

The first day's practice went well. Cass and his co-driver were both quick, and Dave and I were going okay, too. We confidently set about making final preparations for the race. (This is when I made one of the biggest goofs of my entire racing career.)

Mike asked me to check the oil level in Cass's car. I pulled the dip stick, and found that it was a slightly low. No problem-, although my mechanical skills were minimal, I was sure that I could easily add some oil. I went looking for engine oil and found a can that looked like racing oil to me. Unfortunately, the can was labeled in German. But, I was not surprised- I knew that Mike had probably bought some good stuff for us to use. The brand name on the can was Motul. That sounded like engine oil to me. Wrong!!!!!

Motul manufactures brake fluid- not oil! I learned this only after I had poured a few ounces into the engine!!!! We quickly drained, and replaced, the oil- hoping that the brake fluid goof would not create any problems. Right!

We left the track late that night- certain that the cars were as ready for the next day's race as we could make them. We had refreshed all the brakes. Fluids were topped up. We'd carefully checked every nut and bolt to ensure that nothing was loose. The engines were running perfectly. There was nothing left for us to do. We were ready to race. As we left the track, I noticed a large thunderstorm looming in the distance, but thought nothing of it. Such storms were common in Florida.

When we returned the next morning we learned that it had, in fact, rained heavily during the night. And, while our cars had been sheltered under our canopy they were wet- wet even internally as the storm's wind had blown water into the open windows of both cars. But, this shouldn't have been a problem- we just went about drying them out.

However, when we tried to warm my car's engine up prior to the race, it wouldn't start. Not again! We were beside ourselves. Mike and Mark tried everything to correct the problem. As it turned out, despite their best efforts, my car would not fire. They tried everything that they could do in the short time before the race began. But, nothing worked. We would not make the race. I was devastated. Racing at Sebring was so important to me. To his everlasting credit, Dave didn't demand a refund on his driving fee. As it turned out, that generous act on his part was critical.

Later, back at the shop, Mike discovered that an electrical wire had been incorrectly run by the original builders of the car underneath the seat's frame. Eventually, over the many races that this car had run, that wire had finally worn bare. And, then, sitting in the rain water that had filled the car, the exposed wire had shorted out the entire electrical system when current was applied to it.

The other car, however, ran very strongly- easily staying in the top ten. The young guy, whose name I unfortunately can't remember, was doing a very good job. Halfway through the race, the car came in to the pits to be refueled, and Cass took over. Gradually, through both pace and attrition, he began to pick up spots. Then, as the race neared its conclusion he moved into fifth place, and was actually closing on the cars in front. We were beside ourselves with joy! A top five in this strong field of cars was beyond our wildest dreams. But, then- only a few corners later- Cass screamed over the radio that something was wrong with the car's engine. Later we learned that it had blown. Instantly, we went from being on top of the world, to being totally devastated.

I've always wondered if residual brake fluid in the engine played a role in this failure. No one has ever blamed me for that- but, I've always suspected that my screw up may have, at least, been a contributing factor. But, blame aside, what was critical was that I hadn't budgeted anything for a new engine- and, I certainly didn't have any money to buy one. At this point the team could very well have folded. Fortunately, my friend Bill Wilkins stepped up with a donation of $2,500 to help cover the cost of a new engine. With that, and with Dave Devaney's contribution, the team was able to continue.

Our second race was the Miami Grand Prix- at that time one of the country's most glamorous and exciting events! The races were run on a course laid out largely within the confines of the City of Miami's Bicentennial Park. The track ran alongside the waters of the Port of

Miami, with cruise ships and palm trees overlooking much of it. Truthfully, it was a gorgeous circuit- both aesthetically, and from a drivers' standpoint. The course was roughly two miles long, and featured tight, technical turns together with a high speed sweeper and a fast back stretch that ran down Biscayne Boulevard. (After all these years it is still one of the tracks that I remember most fondly. I loved it.)

For this race, Mike was teamed with Cass; I had found a young guy from Central Florida who was willing to pay us to drive in the race. He was even less experienced than I was. We decided that he would start the race (it's always good to get the payers' laps in the books to ensure that you will get his fees!). In practice things were going well until Mike managed to back his car into a guard rail. Unfortunately, the car was badly damaged- its frame was actually bent. This type of damage was not an easy thing to fix at a race track. Eventually, we resorted to literally chaining the frame of the car to a stout palm tree, and then rocking the car back and forth until we managed to bend the chassis back into approximately its proper position. Amazingly, this rudimentary repair worked well enough for us to feel that we could race the car.

The next day Cass and Mike, despite having to drive a car that was far from being as good as it had been prior to the crash, achieved a decent finish- a top ten, if I remember correctly. My car was a little bit further back. The paying driver, as to be expected from someone with as little experience as he'd had, was somewhat slow. As soon as he'd completed his necessary laps, we directed him in for the pit stop, and I took his place.

I was so looking forward to driving the car in the race. In practice, I'd loved the track. Granted, it had taken me a while to come to grips with the flat sweeper that led onto Biscayne Boulevard, but once I'd learned that I could do it without lifting, it was fun. But, what I really enjoyed were the slower technical turns. My car was set up perfectly, under trail

93

braking, to rotate as I turned into the tight corners. It felt to me like it may have handled better than any other car on the track. Although I was out of contention, I was proud of my driving that day. And, even after all this time I can say that this was one of the races that I most enjoyed driving!

The intent of this book is not to provide a detailed documentation of all the races we ran. Rather, just to highlight some of my favorite memories and recollections about our adventures and accomplishments.

I recall that because of our engine woes, we had to miss the following race at Road Atlanta. The next race at which we showed up was at the Heartland Park course in Topeka, Kansas- which should you not know is a very long way from Miami, Florida! I had flown up, as had Mike's wife Karen. Mike and Mark, on the other hand, had driven, pulling the trailer. I still remember that when we met Mike at the track he was extremely upset about his experience pulling the trailer behind the Suburban. Apparently, the weight of the rig was too much for the car to safely handle. He described being petrified with fear as he struggled to control the swaying rig as he pulled it through thunderstorms that bedeviled him for much of the journey. He swore that if, by the grace of God, he managed to survive the trip home he was going to buy a proper truck. And, he did. I believe he still owns that same truck to this day!

Another memory of that weekend is of the motel accommodations that I had booked for the team. I had done my best Fodor's research to find what seemed like reasonably priced accommodations close to the track. I didn't have much to go on, but the name of the establishment- The Country Club Motel- sounded promising enough. And, the price was right. I should mention at this time that the motel was located close to a large Air Force Base. Apparently, as it turned out, servicemen may have frequently patronized this classic low rent establishment, sometime booking rooms on a short-term (possibly, even hourly) basis. For whatever reason, I remember that Karen was not at all impressed with the crusty and stained sheets she discovered on the bed in the room to which she and Mike had been assigned. She loudly demanded fresh linens from the startled night desk attendant (who may not have actually spoken English) before she would even unpack her bags. So much for my travel planning skills! But, at least the price was right.

Practice for the race revealed that both of our cars were a little bit off the pace. Granted, none of us had ever seen the track before, but even allowing for that, we were still slow. And, we didn't have a clue why. We were becoming frustrated. Was it our cars? Or, was it our drivers? In desperation, Mike approached our Honda rep, and asked if he could ask one of the fast Honda drivers to take our car out for a few laps. Just to give us an opinion about whether our set ups were in the ball park. To that end, a driver by the name of Lance Stewart, a multi-times champion, agreed to try our car. Within a few laps he was turning times that were essentially identical to those he'd done in his own car. He had a few minor suggestions about how we might tweak the set up, but the point was clear- our problem was not with the cars. We were relieved- I guess.

We had another paying guy driving with us- again I can't remember his name. I do seem to recall, however, that he was not inexperienced, and was actually pretty fast. I believe this may have been a six hour race- for some reason I remember that it was long enough to have to refuel twice. I can't remember who drove with whom in this race. I tend to think that I co-drove with the new guy, and possibly with Mark. I do remember getting to drive the middle stint of the race. When I exited the pits, possibly after a brake pad change, my brake pedal went all the way to the floor. Fortunately, a quick pump restored the pedal, and I was able to continue without crashing before having ever gotten onto the track. Another memory is that someone had either blown an engine, or dumped a bunch of anti-freeze, in Turn One- a tight right/left chicane. I don't think I spun- but, I do remember the track there being impossibly slick. Eventually, I successfully turned the car over, after an otherwise uneventful stint, to someone (probably Mark) to finish the race. I remember that it had begun to rain just as the car exited the pits. I was relieved that I didn't' have to contend with that. Over the next hour the rain grew in intensity. Water had begun to stand deeply on many parts of the track- I can recall tires spinning, and engines revving, as they futilely attempted to simply accelerate down the straight in front of the pits! Mike, by this time was driving the other car.

Again, we were almost in the running- maybe sixth, and tenth, or something like that. But, the water was getting steadily deeper, and the puddles were growing ever larger. Because of the conditions I expected the officials, at any time, to red flag the race. Eventually, when the red flag finally came out, it was not because of the precipitation itself, but rather because of a huge crash that it had led to- a wreck which involved a dozen or more cars in the turn at the end of the front straight. Apparently, the puddles there had finally gotten so large, and so deep, that several cars had simply aquaplaned straight off the track. Then, as following cars tried to brake in reaction to this accident they too slid off the track. Unfortunately, Mike was one of the drivers who were caught out by this situation. He and his car initially slid safely to a stop in the gravel- stuck and unable to move, but otherwise the car was undamaged. But, then a following car went off exactly as he had, and ended up spearing heavily into our Honda. Fortunately, Mike was still strapped securely into the car- and, he was not injured. He'd made a wise decision that it would have been too dangerous to exit the car while so many other cars were spinning off track.

Another race, more damage. But, as they say- that's racing. And, we still had enough funds in the bank to fix the cars, and make another race. The next race on the agenda was at Mid Ohio. My memory is that I helped Mike's wife and his sister-in-law drive the rig from Florida to the track. We made it with no problems. For this race I had signed up another rental driver. This time he was a young African-American who planned to be the country's next Willy T. Ribbs- a colorful, and fast, sports car racer of the day. Supposedly our guy had backing from a wealthy sponsor in Chicago. That part sounded good. The only problem was is that he had no experience to speak of, and, he was, also, **slow**. Very, very slow. Oh, well- we needed his check. He would be driving with me. Cass and Mark would share the other car.

When we arrived at the track we learned that the entry list was oversubscribed. The plan was to limit the number of starters to the 60 fastest cars. In qualifying, Cass had his car comfortably above the cut line. Unfortunately, my times were slightly below the line. In desperation we put Cass in my car for a couple of laps to try to go fast enough to qualify. However, he didn't have enough clear laps to wheel the car into compliance. I remember leaving the track that night in a very disappointed state. However, my mood improved dramatically when we talked with someone at a restaurant later who told us that since there had been some issue with the timing system all entrants were going to be allowed to start. We were in.

Some of my memories of that race include making a phenomenal start. I ran up the inside of the track and passed at least a dozen cars before the first corner. Mark had started the other car. He, too, had a good run at the start, but over did things diving into the corner. The end result of this exuberance was that he slid into another car and busted his car's radiator. It was out of the race, not even having made a single lap.

In the other car, I ran the first segment of the race. Normally, we would have started the renter, but in this case we didn't think that he was up to handling the confusion of a start. He was really slow! I stayed out for about an hour, having a good run. Eventually, however, I slid off the track into the gravel trap at the fast turn before the "Ski Jump" corner.

Amazingly, I was able to drive the car out of the rocks. As it turned out I had driven off the track because my car's left front tire had gone flat. I limped back to the pits where the team changed the tire, refueled the car, and inserted the rental driver.

We were hopeful that he would settle into a quiet uneventful session. But, that fantasy was quickly shattered. He'd only made a handful of slow laps before he radioed in to report that he'd crashed the car. He was able to slowly drive the damaged car back to the pits, but one of the front fenders was badly damaged. The guys set about cutting away as much of the damage as possible. In the process they discovered that there was no damage to the radiator, to the steering, or to any other vital parts. The car could still run. With that information I yanked the renter out of car, and hopped in. There was no way that I was going to let that idiot back on the track. I drove the remaining laps of the race. Of course, we finished many laps off the lead. The only consolation was that our damaged car still racing around the track made the race's TV highlight show. I guess you have to take your glory where you can find it.

My other memory about this race is that I spent a number of weeks getting the rental driver to send a check to cover the damage that he'd done. I think we finally got it. And, no- as far as I know- his racing aspirations never really amounted to much.

But, now it was time for the year's biggest race- the twice around the clock enduro at Watkins Glen, New York! A real 24-hour race- just like the legendary Le Mans!

Given the effort and expense involved in this event we'd made the decision to only run one car. I was fortunate to have been contacted by Ed Dina- a talented New York racer who was looking to pay for a ride. As events unfolded we were very pleased with Ed's pace. He was quick. He drove with us for several years whenever we came to the Glen, or to Lime Rock in Connecticut.

Watkins Glen, at that pre-chicane time, was quite an intimidating track. I vividly remember being badly frightened twice that weekend- frightened as badly as at any other time throughout my career.

The first time I got in the car to practice it had begun to rain. Unfortunately, I had never driven a race car in the rain. I was also on a track that I'd never driven. And, to make matters worse, the moisture in the air caused most of the windows in the car to fog up. I could see out the front, but that was about it. The side mirrors, and the interior rear view mirror, were useless. All I could do was drive where, and how, I was supposed to drive, and hope that others could see a little better than I could. When that session was over, I pulled into the paddock and slowly climbed from the car. Bill Wilkins was there to greet me. He told me later that I was noticeably pale. Yes- I was certainly scared then.

The next time I got in the car was during the race- at midnight. I seem to recall that I had had to fly to Florida because of some banking related reason. Consequently, I had not been able to get any other practice. I arrived back at the track with the race underway. I was pleased to note that we were running well. No problems.

When you leave the pits at Watkins Glen you immediately accelerate through the turn's climbing esses and slide onto one of the longest, fastest straights in racing. At that time, this straight stretched almost a mile. As you approached the end of it the track sloped downward before you reached the braking zone. Our car was doing maybe a 125 miles per hour at this point. When you got to your braking point you touched the brakes, downshifted from fifth to fourth gear, and turned into the banked corner to the right. This almost ninety degree turn was taken, even in our relatively slow Hondas, at nearly a hundred miles per hour. It was at that time an extremely serious corner. Later, this is where J.D. McDuffie was killed during a NASCAR race, and where Tommy Kendal was crippled when a wheel came off of his IMSA prototype. After those events the track was modified with the installation of the "Inner Loop" chicane- a change made to slow the cars before they got to this dangerous and intimidating bend.

That night, I got into the car cold- having been away from the track for over a day- my only practice having been in almost totally useless rain session. I was, literally, still learning the track. But, there was no time for practice now. It was my turn to race. But, I was determined to take it easy. I knew that I needed to work my way into a driving rhythm, and I didn't want to make any mistakes that would cost the team.

In my memory, the sky that night was pitch black- I don't even think the moon was out. I know with certainty that, even with our driving lights, it was hard to see. I cautiously drove out of the pits, and then accelerated through the esses and onto the long straightaway. At the end of the straight, just as I crested the hill, I carefully applied the brakes at what I thought was a safe distance. In my mirror I could see the rapidly closing lights of much faster traffic- Grand Sports cars were probably a good forty or fifty miles per hour faster than our CRX. I decided to let them go by. I didn't want to interfere with their race while I worked myself up to speed. Therefore, I eased the car to outside of the corner, trying to stay off of the normal racing line that carved down towards the apex. I wanted to be polite and let the fast guys by.

Normally, this tactic would have been the safe thing to do. But, that night, after hours of hard racing, the outside of the track was covered in so called 'marbles'- rubber and asphalt remnants rolled up by the tires as they slid around the corner. The reason this debris is called marbles is because if you drive onto them your car will behave almost as if it were driving on a layer of them. And, that is exactly how my car on its cold tires responded. Despite my reduced pace the car spun 360 degrees, and stopped dead in the middle of the 100 mile per hour corner- in the dark, with the engine stalled, in front of rapidly approaching traffic. At that instant my life, literally, flashed before my eyes. While I was trying to get it restarted two cars came flying past- fortunately, they had seen the yellow flags and had been able to react to my presence. Then, a moment later, my engine fired and I was underway again. I managed to finish that stint without any further problems. Some instances make a big impression on you- this one has stayed with me for years.

We managed to finish the race- always a huge accomplishment in a 24 hour race. I seemed to recall that we were in a respectable eighth place.

Some of the specific things I recall about that race were:

: It is extremely hard to sleep during a 24 hour race. At one point in the early morning I curled up in the race trailer for a while. But, even with the doors closed the noise from the track echoed around the inside of the hauler, and drilled straight inside my head. Not much sleep that night. Others, I recall, tried to sleep in lawn chairs in the pits- same outcome.

: I remember the car coming in for a pit stop sometime during the early morning with its front right brake ablaze! Apparently, the brake caliper seals had burned up, and brake fluid had leaked onto the hot rotor. We had to use a fire extinguisher to quench that flame. The only good news that came from that episode is that because of it we again made the race's highlight films on TV. Glory!

: A 24 Hour race is grueling for all concerned. Not only are the drivers exhausted, but so are those working the pits. And, if you are a small team like ours- where most people were performing both duties- after the race you are really tired. Not only have you worked for the 24 hours of the race itself, but you have also worked hours before the race to set up the pit, and to prepare the cars. And, then, after the checkered flag falls, you've still got to tear everything down, load it onto the trailer, and prepare to drive home. Everyone involved has been awake, and working, for 40 hours, or more. I remember Mike becoming so tired during this race that he went into some kind of trance, or diabetic coma. It was touch and go for a while. Eventually, we got him to eat and drink, and he recovered. I believe that Mark and I drove the rig home to Florida. Straight from the track- we couldn't afford a hotel room, and besides, we had to get home to get back to our real jobs.

: If you are going to do a 24 hour race- you had better love racing. You had better really love racing!

I want to finish this chapter with a heartfelt thanks to Mike and Mark Scharnow- and to all the other members of the team- Schunzel, Petit, and Wilkins. None of this would have been possible without the efforts and sacrifices that you made. I love all of you.

Chapter Fourteen: That Was So Much Fun- Let's Do It Again!

When the season ended Cass decided to go in a different direction. He eventually put together a deal to drive the following season in an IMSA sprint race-oriented, production car series. As it turned out, he would win the championship for that series.

Mike, Mark and I (for reasons today hard to comprehend) decided that it would be a good idea to do another season of Firehawk Racing. But, with Cass leaving, and taking his car with him, we now only had one car. We needed another car.

Our first thought, of course, was to ask Honda for a free car. But, despite our efforts of the previous season to represent Honda well, they were not forthcoming with such an offer. They explained that, while they had been pleased with our efforts the previous season, they hadn't budgeted anything for free cars to be used in the upcoming season. In retrospect, it's easy now to understand that at that time they didn't have a car they were anxious to promote on the race track. But, that wasn't our problem. We needed a car.

While we dearly loved our Honda's we decided that we needed to go through the effort of analyzing the alternatives. After creating a spreadsheet that compared the performance of features of all possible options we narrowed the choices down to a new car that Nissan was bringing to market, and to the new Honda Civic Si that Honda had in the pipeline. I mention this only because of one humorous episode that took place during this evaluation.

I had discovered that a Nissan dealership in Miami had an example of the new model on its lot. We decided that we needed to test drive the car to see what we thought. Towards that end, Mike, and, Dan Hiner, a driver who had agreed to do the next full season with us, met with a salesman at the dealership and took the car for a drive. From what I've was later told, Dan really tried to see what the car would do- both down the straight, under braking, and around the corners. It didn't take long for the salesman to demand that the drive come to an immediate end and that those should never again come back to that dealership. Just as well, we couldn't get Nissan to agree to give us free cars, either.

At the end of the day, given Honda's existing level of support, and given the possibility of even more support in the future, we decided to just buy another Honda. I went to a dealership in Orlando, purchased a new car Honda Civic Si, and turned it over to Mike to begin the process of tearing it apart and building it back into a racing car.

This new car looked promising on paper. It was more powerful than the existing CRX Si that we had been campaigning. Otherwise, it was just a slightly larger car. The most exciting aspect of the car, the reason for its increased power, was a newly developed feature in its valve train that Honda named 'V-Tech.' This feature essentially created a variable cam shaft that became more and more aggressive as the driver's demands for power increased. This transformation happened by mechanism that allowed engine oil to hydraulically move a slide on the camshaft from one setting to another. It was a neat system for the highway- low power and good fuel economy around town; more power when you wanted it. We were anxious to see how it worked.

Mike and Mark worked diligently to transform that car. It was stripped of everything not needed for racing, or required by the rules. A roll cage was welded in. The suspension was modified. Soon it was time to do a test. This time we learned from Honda that they had reserved the race track in Savannah, Georgia for a weekend test. All teams running Hondas were invited to attend. Perfect.

My memory is a little fuzzy on this detail- somehow Lance Stewart- ex championship winning driver- had agreed to test our car for us. I don't remember if Mike contacted Lance directly, or if Honda arranged it. Either way it was an inspired decision. We quickly learned the difference between having an amateur and professional driving the car. He immediately began to dial the set up in. A few laps, come in and tell Mike what he thought we should change on the car. A few more laps, and then additional changes. By the end of the day, everyone was tired but the car's time around the track had improved significantly.

One point of interest during the test was that T.C. Kline had come to the track from Ohio to test the new Honda Prelude Si V-Tech that it intended to run in the Sports Division of the Firehawk Series. Honda's representative, Charles Kurnut, was on hand to keep a close eye on how that test went. T.C. had Randy Probst on hand to drive that car. Randy, like Lance, was one of the best professional production car drivers around. T.C.s team confidently went about its business. But, sometime in the early afternoon the team's composure was shattered when the engine on the Prelude unexpectedly exploded.

We could tell, from the worried looks on the part of the Honda guys, that this failure had them concerned. While they didn't share those concerns with us we knew that this failure had taken place in a V-Tech engine. We had to worry about whether there might also be a similar failure in our car since our engine used the same technology?

We had also taken our old CRX to the test- just to have something else to drive, if the truth be told. Eventually, Lance drove that car, too. We were surprised, and more than a little disappointed when Lance lapped as quickly in the CRX as he had in the new car! That didn't really bode well for the coming season.

This season's first race was again the four hour event at Sebring. We were very fortunate to have secured two paying drivers for the entire year: Dan Hiner, from Indianapolis; and Brad Creger, from Charleston, SC and St Croix, USVI. Both were skilled amateurs. For some reason, we also had two other paying drivers for that race- they were both employees of Garrett, a huge turbocharger manufacturing company in Louisville, Kentucky. They were both good guys, but clearly a little over their heads at this event.

My memories of this event are very fuzzy. Some of what I recall includes:

: Our fear about the reliability of Honda's V-Tech system was soon realized. In practice, Brad lost the engine as he accelerated out of Turn 16 onto the long back straight. Honda's onsite rep quickly huddled with us as Mike torn down the engine. Fortunately, Honda had been keeping up with these developments. Another team had already also lost a similar engine that weekend. As it turned out, the Honda system worked fine at highway speeds, but at race speeds it allowed too much engine oil to pump into the valve train and away from the crankshaft bearings. Whenever that happened- kaboom! I remember being livid, and having an irritated phone call with Dix Ericson- Honda's Performance head in California. Somehow they had already realized that there was a serious problem, and arranged for us to get a new engine. They also provided a fix to the problem. The solution was to install a solid metal spacer in the V-Tech mechanism. This fix essentially locked the camshaft into the high output mode, and totally eliminated the need to pump oil from the sump into the head. They also had worked with IMSA to approve this modification. Following this change all the V-Tech engines were super reliable.

: This race marked the first driver death that I'd ever experienced at a track. Mark Kent, a very talented driver and previous year's champion, lost his life in the 3rd turn, during practice. He'd just exited the pits following some work on the car's brakes. When he reached that turn, the brake pedal just went to the floor. Apparently, one of the car's brake pads had been installed incorrectly. The car drove, at a very high rate of speed, headfirst into the guardrail. Mark probably died instantly, but the car flipped completely over the guardrail and into the viewing area, before crashing into a spectator's bus. Obviously, this was a very bad accident. It forced everyone, I'm sure, to reconsider what we were all doing, and why. But, we raced on.

: Our renters from Kentucky were having trouble coming to grips with the CRX- being a number of seconds per laps slow. They asked me to take the car out to explore whether there were any issues with it. Fortunately, I was able to quickly drive several laps faster than they had gone. The car was fine.

The team's next race was at Road Atlanta, a fantastic track located northwest of the city of Atlanta. I'll begin my recollection of this race with a lyric from a song by Mike and The Mechanics (not surprisingly, one of Mike Scharnow's favorite groups).

"Mikey was a race car driver,

He drove so god damned fast.

He didn't always finish first,

But he never finished last!"

I had begun to consider this little ditty as being descriptive of my racing career. I wasn't the fastest guy on the track, but neither was I the slowest- I was just a mid-pack kind of guy. But, I took some pride in the fact that I hadn't finished last in a race.

Dan Hiner and Brad Creger were entered for this race in the Team's CRX (last year's car). They had quickly soured on the new Civic Si. Mark and I were entered in it. But, first I had to come to grips with this intimidating track. In its original configuration (which is what we were running) it had a number of very fast and scary corners. Eventually, with Cass Whitehead's help, I was able to come to grips with the place. As the race played out the CRX ended up finishing in a credible ninth place. The Civic, however, again developed engine problems- after only 4 laps. I finished last! So much for me using this Mike and the Mechanic's song as a theme song.

I have limited memories of the remainder of the season. I remember again racing in the 24-hour race at Watkins Glen. By this time we had decided that the CRX was actually faster than our new Civic. Ed Dina was again driving with us. He was teamed with Mark, and someone else in the old car. I was driving the new car. I also remember that we had a new renter with us for that event- a judge from western New York. Unfortunately, he was extremely slow- in fact, not only was he slow, but his driving was actually scary. He was all over the track- not because he was out of control, but rather just because he didn't really know what he was doing. My recollection is that we let him have one session in the car during the race. Watching him as he drove by we were scared he was going to hurt someone. And, certainly, he was going to compromise our race results in that car. It was my job to relay the news to him that we weren't going to let him drive anymore. That was not a fun conversation.

As the race went on the CRX continued to move up in the standings. Around mid-night, as I raced around the track in the Civic, I recall hearing over the in-car radio that the CRX had just moved into the class lead. That was the first time we had ever led any race. I was ecstatic. The Civic was running well, too. Unfortunately, only a few laps later the track went to a full-course yellow status. The report was that a car was on fire. Yep- it was our CRX. The engine had blown as Ed raced into the section of track known as the 'heel of the boot.' The oil from the hole in the block poured onto the hot exhaust headers, and ignited. It took quite some time for the track's safety team to extinguish the fire. I recall driving around under caution for many laps. At that time I had no idea that the burning vehicle was ours. Ed, understandably, had exited the car as quickly as he could to escape the flames. Therefore, he had no radio communication back to the pits. But, soon enough we learned the truth. So much for leading a race!

Following the retirement of that car we began to put our faster drivers into the Civic- I think I did one more stint in the car- but, it made more sense to have Ed drive the car than me. He was several seconds per lap quicker. I have memories of working with Mike in the pits to plan our pit stop strategy for the remainder of the race. Essentially, we worked backwards from the scheduled conclusion of the race to ensure that we didn't make any more stops than necessary. As the race neared its conclusion that strategy work paid off as we were able to pass a car that pitted and moved into fifth place- where we finished. We were very excited with a top five finish! This was big time- as far as we were concerned. From then on anything less than fifth place was a disappointment.

The next race that I recall was at Road America in Wisconsin. This circuit is an amazing four mile long track, with a history, like Watkins Glen, that dates back to the earliest days of American road racing. All of my heroes raced here, and the basic layout of the track is unchanged from what those drivers raced on. It remains one of the best road racing courses in the United States.

There are a number of elements that make the Road America course stand out. For example, it has three different straights where cars reach top speed. I don't know of any other track that can say that. And, all three of those straights lead to heavy braking areas that set-up exciting passing zones. In addition, the course features an array of different types of medium and fast corners. The course incorporates the natural hills and valleys of the area to good effect. But, beyond all of this, the track's defining feature is one signature corner- a turn whose intimidating nature is distinguished by its innocent sounding simple name: "The Kink!"

The course exits "The Carousel Turn" onto a straight section that allows the cars to nearly reach terminal velocity. The moment you drive out of this corner your eyes begin to search down this straight away for the next corner- "The Kink." At the same time, at least for me, and I suspect for most drivers, your gut tightens, you take a deep breath, and you begin to tense up for the challenge of negotiating the next bend. This turn is nothing more than a simple 45 degree corner- its challenge comes from trying to negotiate this bend without lifting off the accelerator, without slowing at all, or at least, slowing as little as possible. This would be difficult enough on its own, taking any corner at 120 miles per hour is hard, but uniquely this corner is bordered closely on both sides by concrete walls and guard rails. If you make a mistake here, you are going to have an accident- and, if you do, it will be massive.

Some drivers like to brag that they could take this corner without lifting. Not me. I'm man enough to admit that I could never do it. I learned that, for me, the best way through this corner was to lift off the gas slightly as I turned in, and then immediately go back to full power as I entered the turn. This "confidence lift" tactic might have cost me a mile per hour, or two, down the long straight that came next. But, to me that was how I had to do the turn. Like Fernando Alonso said this year at Indianapolis- my right foot just wouldn't listen to my brain. Despite how many times I promised myself that I was going to not lift for this corner, I never could to it. That, my friends, is "The Kink." It remains the same intimidating challenge to this day.

I seem to recall that for this race I drove the CRX with Brad; Dan drove with Mark, I think. We both finished. They were fifth, while Brad and I were thirteenth. Now, it was on to the West Coast.

Our next stop was at Laguna Seca, the famous California track outside of Monterey. I remember only a couple of things about this race. One, Mike and Mark drove together in the CRX; Dan and Brad teamed up in the Civic. Both cars did well, finishing in the top ten- but, neither really challenged for the lead. We were still stuck in the also run category. This was beginning to get frustrating.

The night after the race, while relaxing in the hotel's pool, I remember thinking about what we were doing- and why, despite our best efforts, we weren't yet winning. As I thought this through it finally sank in that if we were ever going to succeed in the high level professional series in which we were racing, everything had to be done perfectly. The cars had to be perfect. The engines had to be perfect. The pit crews and pit stops had to be perfect. Strategy had to be perfect. And, the drivers had to be perfect. As I floated in that heated pool with my head sticking up in the cold Pacific coast air it finally dawned on me that we couldn't win until we had all these elements in place. And, as I analyzed the situation further, I realized that the one element where we needed to make the most progress was in the driver category. To win we would need to do something differently.

My daughters Jamie and Katie had flown with me to the West Coast. In addition to attending this race we took the week before the next race to tour much of Northern California and Oregon. After the race we drove down through Big Sur, and then on to San Luis Obispo to tour the Hearst Castle. Over the next several days we gradually worked our way back to the north. Our route took us next to San Francisco, then along the beautiful northern Pacific coast, and finally turned towards to the northeast to cross through the region's redwood forests. It was a great trip.

The next race was in Portland, Oregon. I drove with Mike in the Civic, while Dan shared the CRX with Brad. The older car finished in seventh, while the Civic came home eleventh. The only race highlight that I can recall came from me somehow managing to spin the car (twice, if memory serves me correctly) coming out of the last corner onto the front straight. Well, at least I was pushing- trying to erase my normal two seconds per lap deficit to the leaders. No matter where we went, it always seemed that I was two seconds slow. Two lousy seconds from glory!

Chapter Fifteen: Thank You, Baby!

Along about this time, I had divorced and had begun dating a beautiful lady (Sherry Giachetti) who would, a few years later, become my wife. We were both going through transitions from failed first marriages. As we fumbled our way along trying to discover what we were going to do with the rest of our lives we found that we very much enjoyed each other's company. We quickly fell in love. Thankfully, we still are today.

Sherry was rapidly thrown into the deep end of my racing world. Fortunately, it quickly became obvious that she enjoyed being involved in it as much as I did. Since that time she has resolutely stood by my side, up to her elbows in grease, dirt, gasoline, and brake dust, as I drove cars around in pointless circles. She has timed cars on the track for hours on end; she has stood alone in the pits as I've happily sped by on the track; she has cooked and catered for the teams; she has entertained track guests and relatives; and, bless her heart, she has endured many years of anger, self-doubt, mistakes, recriminations, yelling, screaming, crashes, arguments, over spending, and other racing-related episodes of me, in general, carrying on badly. She's always been an important, critical part of the team who has always enjoyed going to the track as much as I have.

Chapter Sixteen: Hurricane Andrew

That second year the team was racing at Road America. We were starting to feel pretty good about ourselves. We weren't going to win a race- but, we were now part of the scene. Honda knew who we were, and were giving us a little of their attention. Things were looking up. But, two things happened that weekend that deserve special mention.

Lodging is always a problem around Road America- the small Wisconsin town where the track is located doesn't offer many hotel rooms. And, when the racing circus comes to town it is a struggle to find a place to stay. As usual I was in charge of making reservations. In those pre-web days we had to rely on travel books to discover what was available. For some reason that I can't remember at this time I managed to book the team into a bed and breakfast-like small luxury hotel. The only catch was that it was located in a small town roughly sixty miles from the track. It was certainly not the kind of place where struggling race teams normally stay.

The night after the first day of practice, we were feeling good. So good, in fact, that we staged an impromptu open road race as the team drove our two rental cars back to the track. I seem to recall reaching speeds in excess of one hundred miles per hour- but, that's neither here nor there. More to the point is an event that happened after dinner that night. Mike, Dan Hiner, Schunzel, and I decided to leave the hotel to have a couple of drinks in a nearby bar. For some reason, about half way in the walk to that establishment I decided to bail on this expedition and returned to the hotel. Perhaps I should have stayed- I might have been a moderating influence. As it turned out, one was certainly needed.

Prior to that time, alcohol had never been much of a subject of concern for our team. But, for some reason (probably because things were going so good at the track that we finally had time on our hands!) For whatever reason, Dan, Mark and John Schunzel had decided after dinner to go down the street to a nearby bar. That, of course, would have been fine, but after that they then decided to also visit all the other bars in town. I didn't know any of this at the time. All I knew was that they did not make the scheduled early morning team breakfast. Mike and Brad, who were sharing rooms with some of the revelers, only knew that their bunk mates had suggested that we should go to the track without them- they would come later in the other car. But, that was no big deal. We were in good shape at the track. The cars were prepped, and ready to go for that morning's late qualifying session. We had time to spare. The only potential issue this created was that both of the drivers of our lead car were not yet at the track- Mark and Dan has been assigned to drive the CRX. Brad and I were assigned the Civic. All we could do was to wait and see when, or if, they showed up.

And, we waited. And, waited some more. Finally, with only about 30 minutes to go before the session was scheduled to start, they arrived. I was expecting them to both be bright eyed and bushy tailed- ready to go after a good night's sleep. Instead, what I saw were guys that were clearly hung-over. We early risers began to seriously question whether they could, or should, even drive. Someone had told me that they thought Dan might still be drunk. Dan, on the other hand, insisted that he was good to go. He was adamant that he wanted to qualify. The decision was left for me to make. I questioned Dan, and observed him, closely. I concluded that he wasn't still drunk, and that he was fit to drive. As it turned out, that assessment proved correct. Dan, while clearly not feeling well, managed to go faster than he had in the previous day's practice sessions. But, he was good for nothing at all the rest of the day. As a team we learned something that weekend about Dan- he actually was struggling with a drinking problem. But, to his credit this was never again an issue when he drove for us.

A much more consequential issue took place at the conclusion of the weekend. Mike, Mark, and John, of course, were all from Miami. When they had left town in the middle of the week there had been little concern about the potential for any kind of tropical weather to impact the area. But, as the week had passed, that situation changed- dramatically. They, of course, had been paying more attention to these developments than me. I, essentially, was unaware of what had been taking place. But, they were beginning to become concerned, as were their families at home, about a rapidly strengthening storm now named Andrew. The Miami guys even had some conversations about whether they should bail on the weekend, and fly home to be with their wives and kids. But, at that point, the storm was still only forecast to be a weak hurricane. And, everyone had been through those before. But, overnight the situation changed- Andrew had hit the warm waters of the Bahamas and exploded into a major storm. Ominously, it was projected to become even stronger. There was no question now-the guys absolutely needed to get home to be with their wives and kids. The only problem was that the airports in the area were already closing. It was no longer possible for them to fly home. Their only option was to drive to Miami with their truck, pulling the team's trailer with our cars in it. But, they were in between a rock and a hard place. If they left before the race, it was likely that they would arrive during the middle of the storm. And, everyone knew that all the roads into Miami were already closed. If they left now they wouldn't be able to get anywhere near their homes until sometime until after the storm had passed. If they waited to leave until after the race was over, their families would have to go through the storm without them. But, in the final analysis, there was nothing that the guys could do about that- they would get home the same time regardless if they left before, or after the race. So, we raced- but no one's heart was really in it. Our thoughts were all much further south.

Once the race was over, we packed the trailer as quickly as we could and headed back to the hotel for the Miami guys to check out early. They were on the road south as quickly as possible. By this time we all understood that Andrew had grown into one of the strongest hurricanes on record. It was now a monster Cat Five storm headed straight for the south side of Miami- headed directly at Cutler Ridge and Homestead, the neighborhoods where most of the team's members lived. And, there was now absolutely nothing that any of us could do to help their families who were on their own trying their best to prepare for the approaching storm.

The guys drove home without stopping, except for fuel. They pushed the rig as fast as they dared. They arrived shortly after the storm had passed. It was immediately obvious that the area had suffered a catastrophe. The streets were dark, and most were blocked with fallen trees. No traffic signals remained. Neither were there street signs. In fact, there was nothing recognizable of the gorgeous area they had left only a few days before. And, none of them had heard anything from their families. As they attempted to drive further south towards their homes they were stopped by armed National Guard troops, who were patrolling to prevent looting. The situation did not look good. Eventually, they were able to get permission to drop the rig at Mike's lightly damaged home in Coral Gables, and then were given passes to drive further south to look for their families. It took hours in the black night for them to drive the few miles to their neighborhoods. And, what they found when they got there was heartbreaking. Both, Mark's and John Schunzel's homes were completely destroyed. The houses' roofs were gone, and most of the interior walls were blown out.

Mark's wife, Dawn, and their two children had elected to ride out the storm further south with Mark's parents in Homestead. Unfortunately, that house had blown apart, too. The five of them had survived by hiding in the garage, and locking themselves in the family Volvo, as the rest of the house disintegrated. Miraculously, they all came out of the storm uninjured. The same for John's family- they had almost nothing left, but at least they were alive. Racing suddenly wasn't all that important. Needless to say, our season was essentially over. (Two months later we somehow managed to enter the season ending 12 hour race at Sebring- but finished an uninspired fifteenth, and twenty third.)

We quickly turned our attention to doing what we could to help the guys in Miami. Two days after the storm Bill Wilkins and I loaded his truck with everything we could think of that might help. Tarps, ice, gasoline, chain saws, food- anything we could put our hands on that they might be able to use. We drove down as quickly as we could to deliver the supplies. What we saw when we got there stunned us. It looked as if a nuclear bomb had exploded south of Miami. Nothing familiar remained. We were at a loss to understand how anyone could have lived through that disaster. But, fortunately, most of the residents of the area had survived. The loss of life turned out to be remarkably small. But, the damage that had been done was simply unimaginable. We knew that it would take years, maybe longer, for the lives there to begin to return to normal. Our hearts went out to our friends and their families. It was a long, and silent, drive home for Bill and me.

Chapter Seventeen: Our Championship (Almost) Year

For the next several months there was little thought given to racing. Mike, Mark, and John were simply focused on survival. For weeks they had depended on FEMA for water, and food, and had slept in what remained of their destroyed homes. Eventually, FEMA erected mobile homes on their properties so that they would have a decent place to live while they attempted to rebuild their houses, and their lives. These were very tough times. But, somehow they lived through the experience.

Unfortunately, the same couldn't be said for everyone's marriages. Mike's was the first to fall apart. Soon he was living in what remained of a bedroom in Mark's destroyed home. In less than a year the marriages of just about everyone on the team- me included- had come apart. The stress of the storm, and the stress of racing, had taken its toll. But, despite all of what had taken place, miraculously, the urge and the will, to race remained alive in the team. Today, looking back on those times and that situation, it's hard to understand, but for some reason everyone on the team decided that as soon as they could get their lives stabilized we really needed to go racing again. As a word of caution, I would just say that's that what racing can do to people.

Following the decision that we should race again, I asked for a formal team meeting. We needed to make some decisions about where we wanted to go with the team, and how could we get there. Together we had enjoyed two great years of racing at legendary tracks around the country; we had done things that we'd never dreamed that we would have ever been able to do; and, we'd had a lots and lots of fun. But, none of us were really satisfied about what we'd accomplished- we'd not won any races. Other than leading that one time at Watkins Glen, we'd not even come close. And, what we'd been doing had certainly taken a toll on our lives and relationships. We needed to make some decisions about what we should do next. Towards that end, John Schunzel arranged the use of a conference room in a building for which he was the property manager. We met early on a Saturday morning, and talked.

Among the other things we did that day was conduct a thorough SWOT (Strength, Weaknesses, Opportunities, and Threats) analysis. It was an honest, comprehensive, and thorough, review of what we were doing, and what we wanted to do next. Somehow, we came to the conclusion that we wanted to continue Caribbean Motor Sports- but, we all wanted to see it win in the Firestone Firehawk Endurance Racing Series. We agreed that to do that we would likely need to sacrifice most of our own driving ambitions, and instead, direct our efforts towards the success of the team. We knew that we would need one car organized for the purpose of generating funding for the team; the other car would be focused on winning. To do that, we would need at least one professional driver. We also knew that we would need new, faster cars. The CRX was obsolete, and the Civic simply wasn't quick enough. But, we were hopeful that Honda would be helpful in that regard. We left that meeting focused on the coming year. Mike, however, expressed reservations about just how active he would be able to be in the coming year given the significant changes and challenges in his life at that time.

Honda, at first, was not confident that it would have any cars available to share. The company's commitment to show-room stock racing in the US was being reviewed, etc., etc... But, a month or so later that situation dramatically changed. Mike received a call from Dix Erickson advising him that they would shortly be sending us two new Honda Prelude Si's. The only caveat being that when we were finished with them the cars could not be sold- they would have to be returned to Honda. We, of

123

course, were overjoyed. The Prelude had proven in the previous season, in the capable hands of Lance Stewart and Mitch Payton, to be the fastest car on the track. We knew we needed this car to compete. We quickly put our existing cars on the market- and both soon sold.

In the meantime, I began making calls to try to put together our driver package for the coming year. Dan Hiner still wanted to be on board- but he wanted to be teamed only with fast drivers. He, too, wanted to win. Brad Creger had decided to drop out- he wanted to move on to faster and more exciting cars. Eventually, he was able to do that- quite successfully. He even managed to compete successfully in the Sebring 12 Hour! We were proud of him.

Anyway, at this point we needed to find some drivers. With respect to a professional driver I was initially at a loss. Pros cost money- which we clearly didn't have. But, somehow I began talking with Mitch Payton- the owner/driver of the fast Prelude in the previous season. Possibly, Honda had put him in touch with us. Mitch indicated that he was potentially interested in racing with our team, and that if we reached a deal he would provide his car, and his co-driver from the previous year- multi-time champion, Lance Stewart. For those who may not remember- Mitch Payton was the paraplegic driver who had flipped T.C. Kline's CRS three years earlier at Watkins Glen. It's funny how things develop in racing. One lesson to take away from that- never, under any circumstances, burn any bridges in racing.

Mitch Payton had become paralyzed, as a California teenager, riding a motocross bike. He had crashed and broken his back. Most would have likely given up at this point. But, Mitch, rather than turning totally away from his motocross dream focused on tuning engines for those types of bikes. In time, he created Pro Circuits- one of the most successful companies in the world that specialize in after-market products for motocross bikes. He also owns one of the most successful motocross racing team in the US, having more championships to its credit than any other. To this day his company is still winning races and championships. Mitch Payton is a genuine legend in the world of motocross. Eventually, I guess, his unsatisfied need to drive competitively led him to racing cars. Towards that end he developed a hand control system that allowed him to successfully race a manual transmission car, and secured IMSA's approval to utilize the system in its races. With this system, one lever applied the brakes, while a motorcycle-like twist throttle on another handle controlled the engine's speed. The final aspect of the system was a button on top of the transmission shift lever that hydraulically controlled the car's clutch. Mitch had proven over the previous seasons that not only did this system work flawlessly, but that, when using it, he could drive very, very quickly.

At that time I knew nothing about what Mitch had accomplished with Pro Circuits. Little did I know that he was, even back then, essentially the motocross equivalent of Roger Penske. All I knew was that he was paralyzed, but that he could still drive a car quickly. Looking back on Mitch's possible motivation for considering joining forces with Caribbean Motor Sports I can only imagine that the options for running his single car team had proven to be limited. In the previous season he had employed a very experienced crew chief/ mechanic by the name of John Torok. But, for the coming season, for whatever reason, John would not be available. Eventually, after some prolonged squabbling about money, Mitch agreed that he and Lance Stewart would race with Caribbean Motor Sports in the coming season. We would use Mitch's car which we already knew was fast. We could keep half of any prize money, with the other half going to Lance- and, all of Honda's matching payments. Payton would help out only to the extent extra funds might be required to run his car. I have to come realize as time as passed that the deal we struck was that Mitch would race for free. He always was very, very, very shrewd! Me- not so much.

But, regardless- suddenly, we had winning cars, and winning drivers. And, in Dan Hiner, we had one paying driver lined-up. Now, all I had to do was to find another. Ideally, we could find a reasonable talented driver who was willing to pay for the season. My experience had shown that this particular combination was not easy to come by. Then, one night my phone rang, and I found myself talking with a polite gentleman, with an accent, who identified himself as Fran Broadfoot. He indicated that he was a Canadian, with a fair amount of racing experience, and that he was looking for season long ride in the Firehawk series. We agreed to meet the next weekend at his condo in Ft. Lauderdale.

Sherry, her young daughter, and I drove down to Miami to help Mike and Mark as they worked on converting one of the new cars from Honda into a proper racing machine. I should mention that this work was all being done in the uncovered driveway of what had once been Mark's Cutler Ridge home. We stopped by Ft. Lauderdale on the return trip, introduced ourselves to Fran and his wife, and went to lunch. Apparently, Fran was convinced enough to agree to race with us at Sebring- and, to consider, depending upon how that went, to racing with us for the season. I was excited. Caribbean Motorsports linking up with Fran had immense potential- he had lots of money, he and I hit it off, and he wanted to race with us! This could, and should, have turned into something so much better than it did! All these years later I can only blame myself, my stupidity, and my inexperience for how our relationship actually turned out. (Fran died of a brain aneurism several years after we'd stopped racing together. I'm sorry now that I never actually apologized to him. I wish that I had.)

Chapter Eighteen: Making a Good First Impression!

Sherry, Anna and I met Fran at his expensive high-rise condo that overlooked Ft. Lauderdale Beach. I was impressed- I could smell serious money. After introductions, Fran and his beautiful wife walked us nearby to one of their favorite lunch spots- which, of course, also overlooked the beach. We had a pleasant meal and, long- story- short, Fran agreed to drive with us at the season's first race- once again, the 4-hour event at Sebring. I had tried to sell him on the idea of being paired with Dan Hiner. To me, this arrangement sounded perfect. Dan had money, and was quick on the track. Fran had money, too. He also seemed to be an experienced racer. To me, this seemed like a great pairing. Fran could start the races- using his experience to drive carefully; Dan would then take over for the finish- using his speed to move up for a decent finish. Fran, at that initial meeting, had indicated that he really wasn't all that concerned with being fast, or even with finishing well. Rather, he said that he simply wanted to have a good time on the track. Dan, I knew, wanted to be fast, and possibly win. Essentially, he was a young guy who wanted to make a name for himself. I should have picked up on this critical difference in expectations at that time. But, unfortunately, I didn't. Fran had no delusions about his driving skills- he understood that he was a slower, older guy, with nothing to prove to anybody. He just wanted to race, and have a good time. I was too stupid, too hungry for money, and too desperate to understand that this deal probably wouldn't work. Rather than recognizing and admitting the obvious conflict in expectations, I tried to convince Fran about this pairing's potential. I could sense, even at that first meeting, that Fran was not convinced. But, in the end, my enthusiasm, I guess, carried the day. We shook hands and agreed to next meet in Sebring.

Bill Wilkins and I met Fran at a chain steak house in Sebring for dinner the night before the track opened. The most memorable part of the evening is that Fran drove up in a long, classic, tail-fin bedecked, cherry red, 1960's vintage Cadillac convertible- top down, of course. Fran, obviously, was into having a good time. We spent a lot of time that evening discussing his collection of classic cars that he garaged in the parking deck of the condo where he and his wife spent the winter. I will be the first to admit that I wasn't used to this kind of money. And, I clearly didn't understand the expectations that tend to go with it. I should have paid more attention. But, I was, of course, too concerned about racing, and, critically, about how to pay the team's racing bills!

This year the team's focus was on finally winning a race- possibly, even winning the championship. For the first time we had a proven winning car and driver combination. Lance Stewart was a multi-time professional champion, and Mitch Payton, despite having to drive using hand controls, was plenty quick. We knew that with their car we would be in contention at the front. As a team we came into the race feeling, and looking, good.

Up to this time, to cover our cars in the paddock we had relied upon a homemade metal framework to which we would bungee cord a large blue plastic tarpaulin. While this arrangement was effective it was decidedly down market from the canopies that most of our competitors were using. In the off season, Mike and I had decided that, given our team's newly achieved status, we should significantly upgrade our team's canopy. Towards that end Mike had purchased a large, professional grade 4-car canopy system. I don't actually think either of us truly appreciated just how large, and how heavy duty, this canopy actually was- that is, until we tried to assemble it at the track for the first time. It took many hours to get it erected. I seemed to remember that it took until well after dark to assemble this behemoth. But, once it was up, I have to admit, it did look good. I should mention that the canopy was designed to accommodate four cars. Of course, we only had two, but still it did provide space for us to arrange tables and chairs for the team and our guests. We were, indeed, looking good. But, given the lateness of the hour all we could do was unload the cars from the trailer and park them beneath the shelter. In retrospect, an event during the next morning's early first practice showed that we would have been better served spending less time setting up the tent, and more time on the cars.

For some reason, I decided that Fran should be the first driver to go out in the team's second car. Whether this upset Dan, I can't remember- probably because I didn't have time to pay attention. We had enough to do just to get the driver's buckled in and onto the grid before the session began. Ordinarily, we would have given all the cars a thorough inspection before any session. But, this morning we didn't have time, and besides, I knew that Mike and Mark had the cars very well prepared. The car that Fran and Dan were to drive was brand new- they'd labored long and hard on it in the open sun-baked driveway of the destroyed Cutler Ridge home to convert Honda's gifted Prelude into a competitive racing car. The fact that they were able to do this was a near miracle. The fact that we were even at the track was astounding.

Our lead car carried the number "17." The second car was numbered "18." They were both painted black, with bright tropical accent colors on the bumpers and hoods. The team was proud as our cars began that first practice lap. Caribbean Motorsports had come a long way from its humble beginnings. We were also curious, as the first flying lap began, about how our new driver was going to perform. We badly wanted, and needed, him to be competitive. We didn't have long to wait.

Fran came down the front straight at speed. He wasn't hanging back. He looked confident. That was good. He properly positioned himself to make the turn into the high speed, left-handed, corner that is Sebring's Turn One. The speed approaching this corner is approximately one hundred twenty miles per hour. To prepare to enter the corner the driver brakes lightly, shifts to fourth gear, turns in, and nails the power. Fran did all those things properly. But then, for some unexplained reason, the car' tail snapped into a high speed spin, rotating violently before slamming hard into the outside tire wall.

We were devastated. Only one lap into the first practice session of the season our new driver had badly damaged our freshly built race car. At that point everyone assumed that our driver had made a mistake. The race was red flagged while the safety marshals checked on Fran, and removed the car from the track. I seemed to remember that Fran was taken to the infield care center to be evaluated. A few minutes later a wrecker drug the damaged remains of the number 18 to our paddock and dropped it. We rapidly pushed it under the canopy and began to evaluate the damaged car. One of the first things we did was to look under the rear of the car at the suspension. We couldn't understand why the car had spun the way it had. Had the suspension failed? Was something broken, or was there something loose? But, we couldn't see anything out of line. The tires and wheels looked okay. We were at a lost for what could have caused the spin. Maybe it had been the driver's fault. We set about repairing the crash damage to the rear bumper and fender. It would take some work, but we knew that it could be fixed in time to make the qualifying session that afternoon.

We already had most of the damaged parts removed by the time Fran arrived. He was uninjured- but, he was clearly shaken by the experience. When we asked him what had happened in the crash he said that the tail of the car had simply rotated as soon as he had turned into the corner. He had never experienced anything like it. He wanted to know if that was normal for how we set up our cars. We assured him that it wasn't. While we did like the cars to be able to rotate- otherwise, the front wheel drive cars would have too much under-steer to corner quickly- but certainly not this much. We could only guess that, somehow, we had set up the new, untested car too loosely. We assured him, that we would make some adjustments to correct the problem. Actually, we were now worried about his driving- while he was worried about whether we actually knew what we were doing. On top of this, Fran was extremely disappointed with the cleanliness of the inside of the car. He took me over and pointed inside it. It was, indeed, filthy. Dust was everywhere. This was, of course, not all that surprising given that the car had been sitting outside for months in the dust and grime of hurricane ravaged South Florida. Mike and Mark had simply been too busy to worry about this issue. But, Fran certainly had a valid point. We all knew that race cars should be, needed to be, spotless. We promised him that we would remedy the situation.

Fran sat down in the shade of the canopy to cool off, and to settle his nerves. Sherry and I went to work on the car's interior, while Mark and John continued to repair the crash damage. Both teams made good progress. By the time Sherry and I stood outside the car to admire our handiwork, the other guys had decided to look inside the rear trunk of the car to see if anything there had been damaged. But, they only lifted the lid for an instant before slamming it shut. They then quickly waved at me to join them in the trailer. They grabbed Mike, too. We all four huddled together inside for a hushed conference- away from where anyone else could see or hear.

Mark and John were nearly breathless. I could tell that they were worried, and excited at the same time.

John whispered to Mike and me, "We've got a problem- a big problem. We now know why the car crashed. You're not going to believe this!"

"What caused it?" I asked. "Was something broken? Was something not put together right?"

"No. There's nothing like that. It's just that we didn't, I guess somehow we forgot, to unpack the trunk of the car last night. And, we didn't check it this morning before we sent Fran out. It's full of all kind of stuff. There's no wonder the tail of the car took off. There must be three or four hundred pounds of extra weight in it."

"Holy, Shit!" I exclaimed. "We could have killed the guy. How could we have done that?" Mike, Mark, and John just shrugged, and shook their heads.

"Jeez- I don't want Fran to find out that we're that stupid. If he does he'll probably walk off and never come back. And, we can't have that- we need his money. Keep the trunk closed until he's gone, and then clean it out. In the meantime, how's the crash damage? Are we going to be able to fix it?"

Mark answered, "Sure. We're almost done. All that's left is to get a new bumper cover from Honda, and to install it. I'm going down to go get one now. "

"All right, that's great! Mike, how's the other car?"

"There's nothing wrong with it. In fact, I just got the timing sheets and we were the fastest car in the session. All we need to do is wipe it down, check it over, and set the tire pressures. It's good to go."

"There's nothing in its trunk, is there?"

"I'm going to check now," Mike answered.

"All right. Let's go back to work. But, ya'll keep the trunk closed until Fran's not around, and remember- nobody says anything."

"Right," they answered.

A half hour later Fran announced that he was going back to his room to get cleaned up. We sent the ladies off for lunch. No one was left under the tent but Mike, Mark, John and me.

"All right," I said. "Show me what's in the trunk."

John popped the lid. I couldn't believe what I saw- two tire and wheel assemblies, a heavy iron floor jack, a tool chest, a box of iron brake rotors, a cooler, and a shop vacuum! The trunk was filled to the brim with racing equipment and supplies- stuff that the guys had locked in the trunk to provide some security in their open driveway work space. I had been an understandable, if silly mistake. Thankfully, Fran had not been injured. We never did tell him what we'd done- I probably should have.

We spent the next several hours making sure that the car #18 was spotless, and ready to go. Dan was scheduled to drive that afternoon's qualifying session. We were hoping that that session would go uneventfully. But, of course, it didn't.

Dan- I think- was at that time convinced that he could drive as quickly as Lance Stewart. We tried to tell him that he was being silly, and that all he needed to do was drive carefully and get the car in the show. But, I guess in his mind he'd concluded that "To be the man, you've got to beat the man!" He was trying as hard as he could.

Unfortunately, at one point towards the end of the session he spun the car going into Turn Seventeen- the last corner on the track, at the end of the longest straight. He was probably doing one hundred and forty miles per hour at that time. The good news is that he didn't hit anything. The bad news is that as he was sliding backwards at over a hundred miles per hour air pressure sucked the back glass hatch cover out of the car. As it impacted the track it shattered. Unfortunately, we didn't have a spare- neither did anyone else in the paddock. Honda could ship us a replacement but it wouldn't arrive until after the race.

Mike talked to IMSA's tech guys and got permission to fabricate a substitute out of a sheet of plexi-glass. It wasn't ideal- but, after a couple

134

of hours of shaping and riveting it was securely installed. We could make the race.

The other car was on the pole!

Chapter Nineteen: The Highest of Highs, and the Lowest of Lows!

The race was scheduled to run late the next day. The cars were well prepared. We thought we were ready for almost anything. But, the weather forecast for the afternoon was worrisome. It showed that a strong cold front would pass over the track sometime either before, or during, the race. This front would likely bring heavy winds and rain. This is something we didn't need- for a couple of reasons.

Our primary problem was that we didn't possess rain tires for our new car. The #17 came with a set of shaved rains that had never been used. In our two previous seasons of racing we'd never needed rains, so given our financial constraints, we'd not yet acquired a set for our newly built Prelude. But, now, as luck would have it, we needed them. I went to the Firestone truck to buy a set. But, they'd not brought any to the track unless you'd specifically requested them. Which, of course, I hadn't. And, none of the other teams had any to spare. Everyone knew what the forecast was calling for. The #18 would have to race on dry weather tires. The Firestone Firehawk Endurance Series ran on street tires- the only difference between wet and dry tires was that the dries had been machine shaved to a tread depth of only a couple of millimeters. In other words, they still had a tread- it just wasn't a very deep tread when compared to an unshaved, or wet, normal street tire. When I explained the predicament to Fran I can remember that he wasn't happy. He didn't mind racing in the rain- in fact he felt that his careful driving style would give him an advantage. But, he had doubts about driving on the dry tire in what was forecast to be a heavy rain. I tried to assure him that the remaining tread on the dry tires would be sufficient. As it turned out, Fran was correct. More about that later.

The storm arrived shortly after the race started. Mitch Payton in the number 17 car was leading the class, and was able to maintain that position even as the rain began to fall heavier. Shortly, the track was engulfed in the equivalent of a tropical monsoon- extremely heavy rain combined with almost hurricane force winds. It wasn't long before cars were spinning off the track everywhere. Mitch to his credit continued to maintain the lead. It wasn't long before the track went full course caution in order to pull damaged cars off of the track. This condition continued for quite some time, creating some questions for the car's crew chief (i.e., me). Under normal green flag racing the car would normally need to be refueled after approximately an hour. But, now, because so much of the race had been run in the rain, and under the yellow flag, we'd hardly burned a quarter of a tank of fuel. I remember discussing what we should do with other members of the team- and with Charlie Kernut, Honda's Race Engineer who was assisting all the Honda teams at the race. Charlie's correct advice was to leave him out until he started to run out of gas. There was no reason to stop at that point- we were in the lead. As it turned out we were able to continue that strategy for far longer than we ever thought possible- two and a half hours if my memory serves me correctly. At that point, with the fuel almost gone, we brought Mitch in, and turned the car over to Lance- still in the lead! By now, the track had dried and Lance was in a two car battle for the lead. John Greene was close behind him in another Honda Prelude. They ran like that for the next hour- only a few feet separating them. But, we knew that we had another fuel stop to make. Lance, of course, would stay behind the wheel- but the car would have to be refueled. We had made the decision to not stop until we were out of fuel. We had calculated that at that time there would only be about twenty minutes left in the race. The Honda behind us was following the same strategy. At this point Charlie Kernut made another great suggestion. He explained that since there would little time left to run in the race when we pitted, that we would not need a full tank of fuel. He advised that we consider planning to make a timed stop, i.e., calculating how long it would take to get the minimum required amount of fuel to finish the race into the car. Some more great advice- normally we would spend a minute filling the tank- but, in theory we would only need a third of that much time and fuel to finish the race. We discussed the strategy among the team, and agreed to err on the side of caution and add 25 seconds of fuel. We advised Lance of what we were planning, and told him to be ready to leave the pits upon our command. The stop went exactly as planned. We left the pits still in the lead. The following Honda had, of course, done the same thing, and was still on our car's bumper. The race was on!

At this point the pit crew had done all it could do. The race was now up to the driver and the car. Our only real concern was whether there would be enough fuel in the car to finish. I must have checked my math a dozen times in the next few minutes. But, there was no question that we had made the proper call, and that there should be enough fuel to get to the end.

But then, Lance began to worry over the radio about the level of gas in the tank. He kept telling us that the gauge was reading empty- he was very, very concerned that he was going to run out of fuel. I tried to convince him as calmly as I could that we'd done the math correctly, and that the refueling had been executed as planned. I told him not to worry- he'd be okay. But, I must have not been all that convincing- every lap he would renew his concern over the radio noting that the meter was now below empty. All I could tell him was to just drive- there was nothing that we could do to help.

All of us in the team were beside ourselves with worry. Most couldn't even look at the track- preferring to look away while keeping their fingers crossed. Finally, after what seemed far too long, the checkered flag fell and we crossed the finish line. After over three years of effort, Caribbean Motorsports had finally won a race! And, not just any race- we'd won the premier race on our calendar, my home race, at the track at which I'd always dreamed about- Sebring International Raceway. Today, it's hard to explain how I felt at that moment. Clearly, though that was one of the most important moments of my life.

After the flag fell, and as Lance completed his cool off lap, Sherry made her way down from the upper level of the pit complex where she'd been sitting timing the laps for the entire race- throughout the entire deluge, completely exposed to the rain and win. The job she'd done was probably as impressive as anyone's that day. As soon as she came into the pit, we kissed and hugged. Then, we walked hand and hand down towards Victory Lane. The same Victory Stand where, so many years before, I'd stared as an awestruck kid into the cockpit of John Surtees' Ferrari! My feet may have touched the ground- truthfully, I don't remember!

But, we had in fact won the race. Lance and Mitch were on the podium, and were presented the trophy for first place. As Mitch was interviewed I remember that he thanked "the Caribbean guys," and complimented us by saying that this had been the best prepared car he'd ever driven. That was quite a compliment to Mike and Mark, especially considering that all of the pre-race preparation had, by necessity, taken place in the exposed open driveway of Mark's destroyed home!

But, what of the #18 car? Fran had started the race on the dry tires- running carefully towards the rear of the field. But, when the rain had begun to fall, he had begun to experience issues. He wanted rain tires, which, of course, we didn't have. He continued to complain throughout his time in the car, giving lurid accounts over the radio of how treacherous the conditions on the track were. I also think he spun a few times. Needless to say, he resorted to driving very slowly- the last of the cars still circulating. Dan, in the meantime was beside himself with his car being so far behind. After a couple of hours, I brought Fran in and swapped him for Dan. But, there was little he could do to make up the lost time. They finished in fifteenth place. Needless to say, neither of the #18 car's drivers was happy. And, they, of course, were the ones on whose money we were depending to fund the remainder of the season!

But, I'd have to worry about that later- we'd finally won a race. I was as high as it was possible to be. But, that euphoria didn't last long. I was one of the last to get to the paddock area after the race- I'd wanted to soak in all the joy in Victory Lane as long as possible. And, I was expecting to find, and anxious to join, a happy team celebration in the paddock. But, as I walked up to the compound I didn't hear the sound of a celebration. Instead, the paddock was quiet and dark. I could still tell that something wasn't right. As I looked closer I could see that our huge, new, 4-car canopy was no longer standing on the front side of the trailer- in fact, a portion of the tent was now on the roof of the trailer, while the largest portion of it was spread out around the backside of the trailer. The team's victory celebration was over before it had even begun.

We had, of course, taken steps to secure the tent before we'd left. We'd tied heavy steel nitrogen gas cylinders onto each corner- each of them easily weighed at least a couple of hundred pounds. We'd also strapped on a couple of sets of used tires and wheels- adding another couple of hundred pounds. But, these weights had been nowhere near heavy enough to hold down the canopy when the storm's gusts had hit. Dad Scharnow (Mike and Mark's father) and my young daughters had been sheltering in the trailer when the squall had come through. They reported that they'd tried to help hold down the tent, but those efforts had not helped in the least. The winds lifted the large canvas, and in an instant bent the entire assembly backwards over the trailer, throwing the securing gas bottles and tires high into the air. One of the legs of the trailer actually penetrated the trailer, all eight feet being driven inside. It was extremely fortunate that no one was injured during this mishap. We were equally lucky that neither the tent, nor the launched projectiles, managed to damage any of the cars parked closely behind the trailer. Lucky indeed.

It easily took a couple of hours to disassemble the remains of the tent and clean up the mess it had created. It was well after midnight before we were done. By that time we were all exhausted and starved- none of us could celebrate, even if we'd wanted to. Our winning car had been put in custody by the race organizers- being held securely until the scheduled technical post race inspection that was scheduled for Monday morning. But, we weren't worried about that. This car, of course, had already been through three successful teardowns the previous season. And, we were confident that we'd done nothing to cheat.

Mike and I took off work on Monday morning to attend the inspection. Part of the procedure was a tear down of all engines of the cars that had finished in the top three positions. This was a lot of work, but we knew we had nothing to be concerned about in that regard. But, it wasn't long before we learned that the inspectors had uncovered a problem on our car- a problem that threatened to disqualify our car, and to overturn our victory. I was close to being sick to my stomach.

There was no problem with our engine- it was fine. But, what they'd discovered was that there was no hood latch on our car. The engine cover was held down only by two hood pins. A quick inspection of the rule book quickly confirmed that an original functioning hood latch was required. I, of course, had no idea why this equipment was missing. I could only rely on Mike.

Mike huddled with the inspectors, listened to what they had to say, and explained what had happened. In practice before the race the #17 had been black-flagged for its hood not being fully closed. As it turned out, one of our drivers had run into the rear of another car lightly. This contact had slightly bent the hood, and had caused the securing latch to actually prop open the hood. Mike and Mark, in their hurry to get the car back on track had simply removed the broken latch. We'd not had access to a replacement latch, and beside, the two hood pins were clearly sufficient to securely hold the hood closed.

The inspectors left, talked among themselves, and returned to tell us that they remembered the black flag incident that Mike had described, and felt comfortable with his explanation. They cautioned us to make sure that the missing latch was replaced before the next race.

Finally, the victory was official. Nothing was ever easy for Caribbean Motor Sports!

Chapter Twenty: Atlanta Motor Speedway

The next event was scheduled for Atlanta Motor Speedway- using portions of the NASCAR track and its infield road course. IMSA had never raced at this facility, but was forced to do so since its customary stop at the Road Atlanta facility was not possible this year since this track was being reconfigured and repaved.

We, of course, came to the race on a high- we were leading the Championship. But, despite this I knew that we had issues to be dealt with. After the last race, Fran had written me a very lengthy, thoughtful, and intelligent letter that detailed his concerns about what had happened at Sebring, and which questioned whether it made sense for him to continue to race with us. I couldn't argue with much of what he complained about. One of his phrases in that letter was, as far as I'm concerned, a classic in racing. He described our second car operation as being the team's "Feed Bag." I thought that described our expectations for the car perfectly. But, one of the problems, of course, was that Dan Hiner didn't actually understand that this was the role we expected him to play. He wanted to race for a win. We really had an insurmountable conflict- one that I didn't want to face since I so desperately needed the funds from both camps to enable us to race.

So, we arrived at Atlanta with the expectation, on the one hand, that we would continue to win; and, with simmering tension festering beneath the driver teaming in our second car. And, that tension was only going to get worse.

Dan, of course, had raced with us the previous year. During that time he had become friends with the team, and with some of the spouses of team members. As a result, there had begun to develop within the team a rift between those in favor of Dan, and those who supported Fran. This became even more obvious during the practice days prior to the race. A couple of the wives reported to me that they thought they had seen Fran drinking a beer before he was scheduled to get in the car! I couldn't believe it, but I had to get to the bottom of this. At that point I didn't really know Fran that well. I didn't know if he was a drunk, or not. And, two of our ladies said that they had seen him guzzling a beer. So- I confronted Fran, told him what had been said, and asked him if this was true? He was understandably a little upset. He assured me that this was not true. Not only were they mistaken, but he assured me that he didn't ever drink alcohol at all. He suggested that the ladies must have seen him consuming an energy drink- something he did regularly. At that time, energy drinks were not all that common. I accepted his denial and explanation. But, this wasn't the end of the team tension concerning Fran. Dan cornered me after practice- he again had been significantly quicker than Fran- and insisted that he be allowed to start the race. He refused to again race following Fran- he wanted to run with the fast guys at the head of the field. Personally, I was trying to not take sides in this feud. I just wanted to find out a way to keep everybody happy. Fran didn't seem to mind, so it was decided that Dan would start the race.

For some reason we had changed the engine in the #17 car following the race at Sebring. I seem to recall that since we'd had to tear it down in post-race inspection, and since it was already well used from the previous season, Mitch Payton and Mike had made the decision to take it out and have it rebuilt. If I remember Mitch Payton had arranged to have it delivered in a crate to CompTech (a leading Honda-associated engine builder) at the track. That meant, that we would be running one of the engines out of the new Preludes that we'd inherited from Honda. During practice the new engine had performed well. I believe that we were again on the pole for the race. The only issue with the engine that I can recall is that while doing a post-practice fluid check I noted that the engine was slightly low on oil. Mike and I discussed this, and decided that it had probably either been under-filled when it was installed, or it may have used some oil as the new rings were seating during the engines first hard use. Either way, we didn't think it represented a problem- we'd never experienced a Honda engine before that used oil- they were always mechanical works of art. I refilled the oil to the proper level- adding maybe a quarter of a quart- and moved on.

The start of the race looked promising. Mitch had the #17 car at the front, and Dan had the #18 only a few cars lengths behind. I remember the team being excited at this great start. But, that excitement didn't last long- less than thirty seconds, actually. Dan, going into the second corner managed to get pushed off the track and into a guard rail. The car's race was over. In my mind there was little doubt that Dan had been overly aggressive in the car. He, of course, claimed otherwise. Regardless, Fran was now on his way home, without even having driven, before the race was a minute old. I knew, by contract, that I would have to refund half of his fee for the race. Crap! But, fortunately, our other car was doing well.

Very well, actually. Mitch had kept the car near the lead throughout his stint. When it was time to make the mid-race pit stop we knew that once Lance was in the car, if we didn't make any mistakes, he would be able to take the car to the lead. And, that's what happened. The stop went perfectly. If I recall, we changed front tires, refueled the car, and, of course, swapped drivers with no issues. And, as soon as all the other cars' stops had cycled through we were in the lead- and pulling away! Lance was actually dominating the race- I think our lead may have grown to up to a minute. We were beginning to anticipate another victory. But, with less than two laps remaining, almost within sight of the checkered flag, we could hear Lance on the radio reporting that the engine had just seized up. We couldn't believe it- we absolutely had the race won! Obviously, we were devastated. And, we couldn't understand what had gone wrong. But, as soon as we got our hands on the still smoking car it became all too clear. When I checked the engine's dip stick, I immediately discovered the problem- there was no oil left in the crankcase. This stupid engine had used all of the oil in its system- well over four quarts. We'd never experienced a Honda engine using oil before. What had gone wrong?

Later we learned that the "new" cars that we'd received from Honda were not actually pristine. It seems that they had been part of a shipment of vehicles from Japan that had been unloaded onto a dock in New Jersey. Which is where they had been sitting when a strong northeaster had flooded that dock? These cars may have actually spent time submerged in sea water. From that we deduced that salt water had managed to find its way into one or more of the pistons and, once in there, had corroded the cylinder walls above the piston rings. This engine ran great, but apparently it burned a lot of oil. For some reason we weren't yet experiencing this issue with the engine in the #18. Maybe it had been higher up on the dock during the flood.

I do remember, however, being shattered by this weekend's results. No trophy, no points, no money, one wrecked car, and another with a blown engine. Coming into this race we'd been on top of the world- now, we were absolutely on the bottom. Could it get any worse?

Chapter Twenty One: Indy!

The team's next race was in Indianapolis! No- not at the Speedway where the Indy 500 is held, but rather west of town, at Indianapolis Raceway Park. This venerable facility- better known as the home of the National Hod Rod Association's U.S. Nationals, the nation's most prestigious drag race event- had a little used 2.5 mile road race course. This track utilized part of the drag strip, the return and connecting roads, and part of what also served as a parking lot. Not exactly world class- but, a championship race, nonetheless. In addition, the race was scheduled to take place on Saturday night before qualifying for the Indy 500. In addition, there was also a Sprint Car race planned for Friday night at IRP's half mile asphalt short track. I guess the thought was that the two races would attract some of the Speedway's fans who were in town for the weekend.

The first thing about the weekend that I recall is the Dan/Fran conflict finally came to a head. Fran- came up to me before the car had even gone out to practice and announced that he was going home. He'd decided that he simply didn't want to play with us anymore- he wasn't having fun. Great- now what? I was starting to stress about whether we'd even have enough money to get home.

Then, out of the blue, I was approached by Terry Earwood- Skip Barber's Chief Driving Instructor. He'd gotten wind that we needed a driver. He said that there was a local kid at the track who was looking for a seat, and who was willing to pay. Further, Terry said that he could vouch for the guy's driving- he said the kid would do okay. This introduction actually turned out to be critical to the remainder of our season.

The fellow's name was Dan Nye. I later learned that his father had made a fortune finding gold in Alaska. Dan Nye was on his way up the ladder in racing. He'd done well in the Skip Barber Formula Ford school and wanted to experience something else. I quickly decided that we needed him for this race. We'd see where things went after we'd watched him race. I decided that he would start the race. Later, I understood that I might, and possibly should, have played this differently. But, at the time it made sense to me- chiefly because I needed his money! If I had been thinking in terms of the championship we could have started Mitch in the #17 and Dan Hiner in the #18. Then, when it was time for pit stops we could have put Lance in whichever car was placed best, with Dan Nye jumping in the lower placed car. But, truthfully, winning the Championship was the last thing that I was thinking about at that time-having enough money to get home was preoccupying my thoughts.

We were again on the pole for the race. At the green Mitch got away strongly. Coming into the next to the last corner of the track he was in the lead. But, that's as far as he got. I seem to recall hearing that the car was on fire, and that he'd pulled the car off, and that the fire had been extinguished. The #17 was out of the race. But, the #18 was running strongly- about eighth.

Possibly, at that point I should have switched strategy and decided to insert Lance. But, I didn't. In my mind, I was obligated to run Dan Hiner when the car pitted. And, that's what we did. But, even that decision was not without drama.

Dan Nye had done a nice job. He turned the car over to Dan Hiner in a good position. Hiner set about moving up. As the end of the race approached he was in fifth spot. But, then, instead of cruising to the finish, we had to contend with an electrical problem. Dan began to report that the car was periodically shutting off. Somehow, Dan determined that the issue was a loose wire from the switch for the supplemental driving lights, and then had discovered that if he held the connection with his gloved hand that the engine would stay on. So, he ended up having to drive the last part of the race one handed. It was an impressive job- still finished sixth.

Later, we learned that the fire on the #17 had occurred when an metal oil pump fitting had inexplicably ruptured. This failure had allowed oil to spew onto the red hot exhaust headers. Fortunately, Mitch had turned the engine off quickly before it had damaged itself, and he also managed to pull off the track right in front of a waiting fire crew- who immediately extinguished the blaze. Bottom line, not too much damage to the car, but our championship hopes had taken a big hit. But, at least we had enough money to get home.

Chapter Twenty Two: On and On and On!

Our next race was at the Mid Ohio circuit which is located in Lexington, Ohio. This beautiful track is one of the country's premier racing venues. We were excited to once again return to it.

We came into this race knowing that the composition of the driving team in the "feedbag" car had, once again changed. After the race at Indianapolis I had been more that a little surprised when Dan Hiner informed me that he'd run out of money, and consequently would no longer be able to race.

Here we go again, I thought. How are we going to get enough money to be able to race? Fortunately, Dan Nye had agreed to do the next race. With no where left to turn, I called Fran Broadfoot, and explained what had happened. He agreed to rejoin the team for this race.

There are four things about this weekend that standout in my mind.

1. For some reason, as we were preparing the cars before the race, we asked Fran to drive the #18 car around the paddock to check whether something on the car was working. Later, after he'd returned, parked the car, and left, two Ohio Patrol troopers showed up looking for the driver of the #18. And, it was quickly clear that they weren't looking for his autograph- they were actually quite upset. Apparently, Fran may have innocently driven out of the Paddock and onto the access road leading into the track. We gathered from the angry officers' that this was very much against the rules. Fortunately, for Fran, he was then nowhere to be found. Eventually, we promised the troopers that he'd never do this again, and they moved onto to harassing others.

2. The #18s race was, for the most part, uneventful. Dan Nye had a good run, and Fran finished the race. However, as the race wound down we could see that Fran was having some kind of issues with the car. As he'd come out of the final corner and onto the front straight the car was frequently weaving- just not behaving quite as it should have. We had no idea whether something was wrong with the car, or whether this was Fran's driving style. But, still he managed to finish the race. When he finally pulled into the pits after the race we asked him what had been going on, and he explained that hot oil had been blowing all over his feet. Consequently, his shoes had been sliding on and off the pedals. This had to have been disconcerting for sure. Mark looked the car over after the race, but was unable to determine any reason for this problem to have occurred. Maybe, he guessed, the engine had just been over-filled. Right! You are never, ever, that lucky in racing.

3. The #17 car won the race! But, not without a little of customary Caribbean Motor Sports drama. As the last lap started, Lance was in the lead, with several cars nipping at his heels. The next thing we hear, as Lance reached the backside of the course, was that one of those trailing cars had intentionally knocked him off the track. Lance was fit to be tied- he screamed that he'd been taken out blatantly by the following car. He was ready to fight. He rejoined the race in second place, but too far behind to be able to retaliate. Even before the race ended I was in the face of one of the race officials- complaining that we'd been intentionally knocked off the track. I was directed to climb the tower and complain to the Chief Steward- which I quickly did. I should add that up to that point I'd never actually met a Chief Steward before- I really didn't know how to behave. But, regardless, I was still able to get my point across. He listened, and then told me that he was already aware of the issue, and that it was being reviewed. When I asked him what

that meant, he advised that I should just shut up, go back downstairs and wait to hear from him. Which is exactly what I did. Ten minutes, or so, later an announcement was made over the Public Address system that the results of the race had been revised. A decision had been made, after consultation with the corner workers that had witnessed the incident, that we had in fact been unfairly knocked out of the lead of the race. The car that had done that was disqualified, and we were named the winner. We needed that win!

4. We celebrated that night at the largest restaurant in downtown Mansfield, Ohio. All the racers were there. We had a really good time! I remember that John Torok, crew chief on a competing car, hit Mitch Payton on top of the head with a pie pan full of whipped cream. Things kind of went downhill from there. Somehow, Mark Scharnow and I decided that, in retaliation, we should jack up John Torok's truck, which was in the parking lot. Then, we put some jack stands, that we'd found in the bed of his truck, under the rear axle. Not very high, of course, - just enough to insure that the truck's wheels were off the ground- but not so high that he would notice before he tried to drive the truck. I never actually heard how that turned out. We'd left by then. Just racing hi-jinks.

The next race was only a week later- in Watkins Glen, New York- the birthplace of road racing in the United States. I can't remember how the cars and the rig got there. But, they did.

There was a test day scheduled at the track before official practice started. For some reason, Fran wanted to do this day along with a friend of his from Canada. This friend was potentially interested in doing the race. However, the day didn't turn out well. I remember getting a call back in Florida from Fran- explaining that the engine in the car had blown-up. Not only had it blown-up, but he explained that there had also been another oil fire. There was no way that the car was going to be able to race. Truthfully, I wasn't all that surprised that the engine had expired, given how it had pumped out oil at Mid-Ohio. And, remember, this was one of the original engines that had probably spent time being submerged. We all suspected, although we hoped that it wasn't, that the engine was on its last legs. Apparently, the salt water immersion had finally taken its toll on this engine, too.

Fran felt bad about what had happened. Knowing that I needed his money, he agreed to let me keep his race fee if I would agree to return it at the end of the year. Why he did that I'll never know. But, I certainly appreciated it.

The race itself was not one of our finest moments. Early in the race, something came loose on the #17 which necessitated a trip to the pits and caused us to go at least one lap down. It seems like someone may have run into the rear of the car, and the impact had caused the exhaust system to drag on the ground. As the race wound on, and as pit stops unfolded, it became very confusing as to who was running where. Towards the end of the race Lance actually managed to pass the car that was being identified as the leader of the race. I was convinced that that pass made us the leader. But, timing and scoring didn't see it that way. I spent an hour or more after the race pouring over the lap charts of the race trying to understand what had happened. But, bottom line- we finished fourth, not first.

The next race, another week later, was scheduled for the monstrous road course known as Road America. This 4- mile long track is the favorite of every driver in the U.S. We were, of course, looking forward to racing on it. But, there was a lot of work that needed to be done on the cars, and just a very short period of time to do it. To his everlasting credit, Mark elected to take off work that following week, and to spend the time in Ohio getting the cars ready to race. That, of course, meant replacing the engine in the #18 car, and repairing any damage done by the fire. Fortunately, the Ford dealer in Cleveland, our racing friend Dick Ruhl, agreed that Mark could use a bay in his dealership to do the work. Without that generous offer there is no way that we could have made the next race.

I have little recollection about the #18 car in that race. Dan Nye drove again; but, I can't recall who his co-driver was- possibly Mark. Fran- after the last two troubled outings with us had once again called it quits. All I remember about this car's race is that Dan managed to crash it in "The Kink" early in the race. Fortunately, he was not injured.

I do recall very well, however, the #17's race. Some of the highlights were:

- The night before the race the track experienced an unbelievably intense thunderstorm- with heavy, heavy rain and one of the worst periods of lightning that I have ever experienced. And, coming from a Florida Native, that's saying something. We'd worked late at the track making double sure that the cars were in good shape. I remember spending a fair amount of time under the cars safety wiring the exhaust pipes to the frame of the car. I didn't want them to ever fall off again.
- For the start of the next day's race we were once again on the pole. But, on the pace lap Mitch began radioing that the car's engine was misfiring- badly. By the time the race started he had fallen far behind the field. In fact, he was at risk of going a lap down before he could get the car back to the pits. But, then, miraculously, just before he pulled into the pits the engine started

157

to run strongly. He stayed out. The engine ran fine for the rest of the race- but, of course, we were at the back of the field. We decided to put Lance in the car as soon as we could, and during the full course caution caused by Dan Nye's crash, pulled Mitch in to make the driver switch. Soon, thanks to Lance's aggressive driving the car was back near the front. For the last hour of the race Lance, and our primary competitor- John Greene in Mark Hein's Prelude, ran inches apart, with John in the lead. In my mind, at least, Lance was outdriving John, but it seemed to me that the other car had some kind of advantage- either horsepower, or more likely, transmission gearing since Lance and John were shifting at significantly different places as they came up the front straight. Every lap I expected Lance to find a way past- but, that never happened. We finished second-close, but no cigars.

After the race, there was a near fight in our paddock. I missed it, but heard about it later. Paul Hacker, who with his brother Karl, made up the so-called "Hacker Express." They had been racing in this series for years, and had won many races and championships. They were serious racers, for sure. This year the Hacker brothers were running cars in the Sports Division, the next faster class above us. I seem to recall that they had not been having a good year- truthfully, their Oldsmobile's that year were not all that quick. Apparently, Lance in our car, and Paul Hacker, had come to the infamous high speed "Kink" corner at the same time. Lance, being in a **very** big hurry, apparently had ruffled Paul's feathers as they had gone through this daunting turn. Paul may have actually crashed as a result. Regardless, for whatever reason, he was plenty angry at Lance. Lance, for his part, didn't think that he'd done anything wrong. Eventually, someone managed to pull Paul out of our paddock. Just another post race "discussion," or, at least, so I thought at the time.

Chapter Twenty Three: Go West Young Men!

The next two events on the calendar were on the West Coast. The first was at Laguna Seca near Monterey, California; the next was at Portland International Raceway in Oregon. Both were a long ways from Elkhart Lake, Wisconsin. We knew we needed to do these races, but we didn't know how we were going to get the cars and rig there.

Fortunately, and without me even knowing, Mark had discussed our plight with a couple from Virginia who sometimes raced in our series- Richard and Annie Mitchum- and had already solved our problem. They apparently thought it would be a hoot to drive across the country pulling a trailer full of race cars. All we'd have to do is pay for the gas. No way that we could turn down that offer. Initially, they drove to the Los Angeles area where they were able to park the trailer at Mitch Payton's ProCircuit garage. It seems like Mark flew out to prep the cars, with Richard's help. All I know for sure is that when Sherry and I flew out to San Francisco and drove into Laguna Seca the cars and rig were there waiting on us. It was just like we were a big time race team!

We were looking forward to picking up the battle with Mark Hein's team. But, before we could get to that we would have to deal with another issue. For some business related reason Mitch Payton had not been able to make the first day's practice. Therefore, Lance had taken out the #17. But, shortly after he went out the session was red flagged. It seemed that there had been an accident in the "Corkscrew" corner. We were disappointed when we found out that our car was the reason for the flag. It had been involved in a serious accident, and was having to be brought back to the paddock on a flat bed. But, when Lance returned, and we found out what had happened, we were more than a little disappointed- we were pissed!!!! It seems that the Hacker Brothers had chosen that session to take their revenge. They hadn't actually done it themselves, but had gotten their hired gun pro driver (Scott Hoerr) to do their dirty work for them. He clearly, and intentionally, punted Lance at the Corkscrew. The car was badly damaged, i.e. the car's chassis was badly bent! It needed to go to a frame shop to be straightened. Mark and Richard left with the flatbed to go into town to find a frame shop to fix the car. All the rest of us could do was fume, and think about how we should respond. But, since there were a lot more members of the Hacker Team standing around trying to look innocent than there were the few of us trying to look threatening, there was not much that we could do.

The boys brought the straightened car back a little after dark. This was about the same time that Mitch Payton arrived at the track. For whatever reason, he wasn't particularly happy. I do remember that it was his birthday, and we tried to cheer him up by ordering his favorite style pizza that night – I never have been able to understand why anyone likes pineapple on a pizza! Whatever, it was a late night as we worked until the wee hours rebuilding the crashed car. The Hacker Team had by this time been long gone from the track. It was a testament to the character of our team that no one went over to sabotage their cars.

Dan Nye was again on board to drive the #18. But, I had not been able to locate a co-driver who was willing to join the team. Lance put us in touch with an experienced California driver that he had raced against in the past. This guy was a professional- i.e., he wasn't going to pay us to drive. But, we needed a fourth driver. The fellow's name was Luis Sanchez. We later learned that he and his brother, Iggy, were quite well known in the area. Lance had raced with them in his younger days in California. We enjoyed having him with us. He did a great job in the race.

The race itself was not quite what we needed. We ended up finishing fourth in a very confusing, caution-filled race. The #17 car experienced an electrical problem early that caused it to go several laps down early in the race. Because of that we made the decision to put Lance in the #18 car when Dan Nye brought it in. Luis Sanchez would get in the #17. Later in the race another mysterious electrical issue appeared on the #17, and the car came to a stop on the front straight- bringing out a full course caution. But, as soon as the field bunched up behind the pace car Luis was able to get the car re-fired, and managed to drive it back to the pits. Mark and John lifted the hood and looked for the source of the problem. They shook a few wires, but nothing seemed out of order. Eventually, as the officials looked on, we told Luis to go back out to race. The car ran fine for the remainder of the event. (The reason for the second electrical issue remains a mystery to this day. I think Sherry may know what happened- but she's not talking.) The #18 car had been a lap down. But, when the full course caution came out we thought that Lance had gotten the lap back, and had closed up right behind the leading cars. Then, as the final laps played out he was able to pass the three cars in front of him. We thought that we had won another race. But, the official scoring showed us still in fourth place. As I said, it was a very confusing race. Apparently, when the field was under caution the three leading cars had gotten a wave around. Therefore, when we later passed them we were merely getting ourselves back onto the lead lap. Initially, we were very disappointed with these results.

But, as it later turned out, finishing in fourth place was actually a good thing. Prior to the race we'd gotten a Honda transmission specialist to install a gear ratio out of a sports class Prelude into our transmission. Given what we'd seen at Road America we were convinced that this was the secret advantage that Mark Hein's car had enjoyed there. But, apparently, the tech inspectors may have had the same suspicion. For whatever reasons, that is the part that they chose to have torn down during the post race inspection. We were relieved that we'd not had to undergo that scrutiny, and very surprised when nothing out of order was found in Mark Hein's gearbox. To this day I still have questions about how all of this played out.

Chapter Twenty Four: Portland International Raceway

The next race was in Portland, Oregon. Richard and Annie had, to the best of my recollection, driven the rig up. I flew in and met Mark, John, Richard and Annie. For drivers, we had a new pairing in the #18. While we were in Laguna, a young driver, Rich Rutherford, had introduced himself. He was an instructor for one of the west coast racing schools- and, he and another instructor were interested in renting the ride at Portland. I was, of course, delighted. Dan Nye had already told me that his plans wouldn't allow him to race at Portland. We'd never had that kind of combined talent (Nick Harvey, and Rich Rutherford) in our second car.

All of our drivers were very quick in the race. It should have been an easy victory for Lance, but unfortunately, Mitch Payton and I got our wires crossed when it was time for him to pit. I thought that I'd told him to bring the car in under a full course yellow; Mitch thought that I'd told him to stay out. The end result, when we finally got Lance in the car, was that he was at the tail end of the lead lap cars. John Greene in Mark Hein's car was in the lead. Lance drove his best race for us that day. He passed every car, including the leading Prelude. It was another victory for Caribbean Motorsports. The #18 car, finished in a strong third place. We had two cars on the podium, and were on top of the world.

Now, there was only one race remaining- a 12 Hour finale at Sebring International Raceway. Theoretically, we could still win the Championship.

Chapter Twenty Five: Pride Goeth Before the Fall!

The strong result at Portland opened doors for the team. Before we knew it we had an amazing offer in front of us. At Laguna Seca, John Schunzel had been talking with an older fellow from California by the name of Chuck Jones. Chuck Jones had, many decades before, been involved with the American Formula One team- Shadow. During this time, he had become friends with the F1 driver- Clay Reggazoni. Clay, like Mitch Payton, was now a paraplegic. He had been injured driving in Formula One when the brake pedal of his car had snapped off as he attempted to slow for a corner at the Long Beach Grand Prix. But, Clay had not let this slow him down too much. While his Formula One career had ended, he was still an active racer, using his own hand control system. In Italy, even years after his accident, Clay was still a legend- famous, and respected worldwide. Supposedly, according to John Schunzel, he was still sponsored by Marlboro, the cigarette company. John told us that if we could prepare him a car that Clay would race with us, and bring sponsorship of $25,000 from Marlboro! Chuck Jones son, Sean, would race with Clay. In addition, we had several other drivers that had raised their hands to drive with us. In addition to our Portland crew of Mitch Payton, Lance Stewart, and Rich Rutherford, we also now had Dan Nye, Clay Reggazoni, Sean Jones, Dirk Layer, Cort Wagner, and Peter Cunningham.

Peter was a many time driving champion. He continues to be an extremely successful team owner, and driver, even today. Because, we were technically still in the hunt for the series Championship, Mitch had insisted that we hire Peter to drive with us! I seem to remember that Rich Rutherford had introduced Cort Wagner to us. We had no idea who he was, other than Rich had vouched for his talent behind the wheel. We had more than enough drivers for the race. But, now we needed another car.

Which brings us to the second Prelude that Honda had given us before the season? It seemed to make sense at the time, given the number of drivers who wanted to race with us, and given the potential sponsorship from Marlboro, that we should convert this street car, now with a repaired engine, into a race car. Towards that end, Mark, John, Sherry and I spent the better part of a month making that happen. Now, we had three cars entered in the 12 Hour race. Initially, I had assumed that Clay would pair with Mitch and Lance. I thought that would have been a great story- two paraplegic drivers driving the winning car. However, for a variety of reasons that was not to take place. First, Mitch was understandably skeptical- he wanted nothing to do with an unknown commodity in his car. He insisted on having Peter Cunningham in his car. The other issue was that Clay was not familiar with Mitch's hand control system. He had his own differently styled system- it was an electrically actuated device, built by an Italian company named "Guido Electronics.". Therefore, our final driver assignments were:

#17: Mitch Payton, Lance Stewart, Peter Cunningham

#18: Clay Reggazoni, Rich Rutherford, and Cort Wagner

#19: Sean Jones, Dan Nye, Dirk Layer

In theory, this was a strong lineup- especially, if the money came from Marlboro. I kept pressing John Schunzel to make sure that this was going to happen. He repeatedly assured me that it was- apparently, Chuck Jones had told him so. Unfortunately, no money ever arrived- but, of course, all the drivers did.

Reggazoni not only showed up, but, in addition, he brought with him his own two mechanics from Italy. Unfortunately, they did not speak a word of English. They came to the track every day dressed in classic Italian, greasy, brown racing mechanic coveralls. Robert Mitchum quickly dubbed then the "Guido Techs!" They were good guys, who, despite our inability to communicate, were a lot of fun. The reason that Clay had brought them along was so that they could install Clay's custom hand control system on our car. For some reason we had assumed that this system would be similar to the hydraulic system that Mitch used so successfully. But, we were surprised to learn that Clay's system was actually an electronically operated system. There was actually no commonality at all between the two systems, and quite frankly our "Guido Techs" were having difficulty getting their system to work at all on our car. Then, to make matters worse, the night before the race, it rained-hard. Water and electrical components have never been known to go together well. It was a thrash to get the thing working at all the morning before the race.

I learned many lessons that weekend. One of which was to make sure you had the money in hand before any driver ever got into a car. Another was that the complexity, and difficulty, of running a racing team expands *exponentially* as the number of drivers increases. We had been able to run a two car/ four driver team. But, a three car/nine driver operation was another thing entirely. To accommodate this larger assemblage, we'd, of course, brought out the huge canopy again- the one that had blown down at the start of the season. We must have been out of our minds. But, despite all the confusion, and issues, with which we had to deal, we made it to the grid for the race. The #17 was on the pole. But, things went downhill quickly from there.

On the pace lap the #17 began smoking heavily. We brought it into the pits as the race went green. As it turned out the engine's oil filler cap had not been tightened properly- it had been cross threaded the last time it had been put on. Consequently, almost all of the engine's oil had poured out all over the engine bay. We lost an entire lap rectifying this situation. So much for a smooth race. I also seem to remember that Dan Nye, who had started the #19 car, was black flagged for not having any driving gloves on. Inexplicably, he'd simply forgotten to put them on before the start. One lap, and two cars were already out of contention.

However, the #18 car was running strongly. I believe that Cort Wagner was driving. At that time, we had no idea who he was. I do remember, Richard Mitchum tapping me on the shoulder about this time, and saying: "He's a keeper!" Richard was right. Cort went on the have an extremely successful professional racing career- winning races and championships at the highest level. He was very good.

Eventually, it was time for pit stops. When the #17 came in Peter got out, and Mitch got in. He was steadily working his way back towards getting our lap back. But, on a four mile long track that was a very difficult task, unless there were full course cautions. And, unfortunately, there were none. Our plan was to rotate Mitch and Peter in the car, saving Lance until it was clear which car had the best chance to win.

When the time came for #18 car to pit, Cort was removed and Clay Reggazoni was inserted. Because of the difficulties installing the hand controls we had not yet seen him drive. We were curious how fast he was actually going to be. But, quickly, even without practice, he was up to speed- posting competitive times. His pedigree was coming through clearly.

Speaking of Clay, one of my fondest memories of his time with the team was a comment he made following the pre-race drivers' briefing that I conducted the night before the race. I had a list of items that I covered. Rules, pit stop procedures, yellow flags, wave arounds, etc. When the meeting was over Clay commented that the meeting was far better than any he'd ever had when he raced with Ferrari! High praise indeed- I still swell up with pride when I think of him saying that.

Unfortunately, Clay's race was over quickly. After only about thirty minutes we got word that his car's engine had blown. As it turned out, Clay had missed a shift, the engine had revved far beyond its red line, and that was that. One car out. (And, of course, no money from Marlboro!)

The #17 car was running quickly, but it was still a lap down.

The #19 car was having it's own issues. After several hours the car came into the pits with the rear anti-sway bar dragging on the ground. Mark and I dove beneath the car to find out what had happened. It didn't' take us long to discover what was wrong- the weld that held the sway bar bracket to the car's frame had broken off cleanly. I seem to recall that welding it back in place wasn't an option. We may have opted to simply remove the bar entirely. Without this suspension piece the car would still drive- but, it would under-steer. But, we weren't really worried about that since the car was not in contention.

As the race continued our attention was, of course, focused on the #17 car. It was still possible for that car to win- all we needed was for it to get back onto the lead lap. If we could do that we knew that Lance could somehow find a way to get into the lead. But, that full course caution would never come. Hour after hour, Mitch and Peter drove the car for all it was worth. Then, as darkness fell, Peter called on the radio to report that he thought he was beginning to experience carbon monoxide poisoning. He told us that a competitor's car had recently hit our car's exhaust pipe- probably causing a fracture in the exhaust manifold. We told him to bring the car into the pits.

As soon as Peter got out of the car it was clear that he'd been badly poisoned by the invisible gas. His face was literally bright pink. There was no way he could get back in the car- in fact, there was no way that anyone could get in that car and drive it the way it was. Clearly there was some kind of exhaust system leak that was allowing carbon monoxide into the cockpit. We knew we couldn't fix the leak, so in desperation we decided to try to get clean air into the cockpit by breaking out the passenger side window. Towards that end, I directed everyone to stand back, and took a swing with a ball peen hammer at the glass. I, of course, had expected the glass to break, but there was no way that I had expected it to explode into a million pieces like it did!

I seem to recall that I may have installed Rich Rutherford in the car at that point. Peter clearly could not drive, and Mitch was spent. Lance didn't want to commit to driving the car since it was increasingly becoming out of contention. In fact, he had already begun to explore other options up and down pit road- hoping against hope to somehow still be able to win the championship. But, ultimately, he was not able to find a potentially winning car to drive. Therefore, as the race neared its end he finally got in the #17. As it turned out he ended up running in close contact, one lap down, with the cars that were leading the race. He, of course, wanted to pass them so that, if a caution came out, he could get the lap back. They, of course, wanted to keep him behind. Shortly thereafter Lance reported that one of the cars had "brake tested" him going into the hairpin. We didn't know it at that time, but that contact had resulted in our radiator being punctured. A few laps later, our engine over-heated, and it eventually blew up. Our race, and our season, was over.

In fact, for all practical purposes, our professional racing experience was over. We had two blown engines, and practically no money. When our tire bill, and our hotel bill, was paid, there was nothing left. The Marlboro money, of course, had never materialized. Some of the driver's were not happy about paying their bill to us. No one was happy. And, most importantly, all the members of the team were done. We were all tired. We were mostly broke. The marriages of all the key team members had fallen apart. There was no way that we could carry on any further- we were done. Caribbean Motorsports had accomplished a great deal in its three years. We'd all had a great experience, and had gotten to live out a large portion of our dreams. And, we had had a lot of fun. But, now, it was all over.

Mike Scharnow, Mark Scharnow, John Schunzel, Bill Wilkens, Richard and Annie Mitchum, Lance Stewart, Mitch Payton, and Sherry Grant- what you accomplished was nothing short of amazing. With little money, little knowledge, little experience, almost no time, against almost unimaginable obstacles, and with precious little understanding, we were built a formidable, competitive, winning professional racing team. To this day I marvel at what we were able to accomplish with so little. It was all because of your efforts. I love you all. Thank you.

Book Three: Offertorium

"Let the holy standard bearer Michael

Lead them into the holy light."

Chapter Twenty Six: Out of the Ashes

1993 marked the high water mark for Caribbean Motorsports. We ran a few races, just for fun, the next year- but, by that time the team was only a ghost of its former self. I had been given a great new opportunity with my bank, but it required to relocation to Atlanta. Because of that, and other reasons (primarily financial), my racing was done for a while. All the other members of the team were also forced to take a hiatus from racing. But, the smoldering desire to race again never died in any of us. One day (I believe it was in 1995) I got a call from Mike Scharnow. He and Mark had found a race car for sale in an Atlanta suburb, and he asked if Sherry and I would drive up and take a look at it. We were, of course, more than delighted.

As it turned out, Mike and Mark had been thinking about how they could best get back in racing. They, like I, had recognized that a return to the professional ranks was out of the question. They also understood that they were no longer interested in serving in just a support role for other drivers- they wanted to drive themselves.

It is probably appropriate to mention that the brothers had, essentially, been racing all of their lives. They were both multi-time state champions in various karting disciplines. Mike had also spent time after college driving an array of Formula cars- at that time he had aspirations of making it to Formula 1. But, eventually, those dreams faded as the realities of trying to race successfully against hoards of better funded young men became all too obvious. But, the addiction to racing, once it takes hold, is a hard one to shake.

The car that they asked me to take a look at was an SCCA Sports Renault. They had recently attended a SCCA Club Racing weekend at

Sebring. SCCA, or Sports Car Club of America, is the oldest, and largest sanctioning and organizing body for road racing in the United States. The club's roots date back to the foundation of modern road racing in the country. The Club, through its various Divisions and Regions conduct amateur (i.e., club) and professional races across the United States. In Florida, on almost any weekend of the year, there will be some type of SCCA event taking place somewhere. While in the back of my mind I knew this, somehow I had taken a detour around the SCCA by beginning to race with IMSA. At that time, many others did as well. But, now we needed to find out more about how to race with the SCCA.

As I mentioned, Mike and Mark attended a club weekend at Sebring to see what they could learn. I'll never forget Mike describing to me what he'd seen. It was something like- "Mitch- I couldn't believe it. They were sitting around in lounge chairs waiting to go race. They weren't thrashing on the cars at all."

This observation struck a chord with all of us given what we'd gone through each weekend in professional racing where commonly we were at the track, working on the cars, until midnight, or later. And, as they'd toured the paddock, and watched the races, they had been drawn to the class known generically as "Spec Racers." They had correctly noted that not only was this the most competitive class of cars, but more importantly, it appeared as if they were also the cleanest, simplest, easiest to work on, and, importantly, among the cheapest. Furthermore, they'd learned that the SCCA provided support for this class at all events through a network of CSRs, or Customer Service Reps. These CSRs were on hand to provide advice, parts, and even, for a fee, full prep and track side services. Mike and Mark spent a considerable amount of time that weekend talking with the Florida CSR- a likeable fellow named Mick Robinson. Mick's company, Robinson Motor Sports, or RMS, appeared to be a very successful racing prep shop with close to a dozen cars under that team's canopy. Further, almost all the other cars in the class appeared to rely heavily on Mick.

Mike had even chatted with Mick about how he would feel about another company getting into the prep shop business for Spec Racers? As it turned out, Mick indicated that not only would he have no objections to this, he would actually welcome it, since he was the exclusive distributor for parts for Spec Racers in Florida. Mike and Mark were sold. I remember that when Mike called me that night to tell me what they'd seen he was almost incredulous. This class promised an affordable, competitive, relatively easy way to go racing. They were ready to buy a car.

Spec Racers had begun as an SCCA class in 1983 when the Renault company dreamed it up as a promotional vehicle for its re-entry into the American automobile market. The company's thought was that it would design an affordable entry level racing car for the masses that would utilize the engine, transmission, suspension, and brakes out of its "Le Car" economy car. Towards that end it tasked its employee Roy Lunn to design the car. Now mind you, Mr. Lunn was not just any car designer. He had already made a name for himself by designing the world conquering, Le Mans winning, Ford GT40 for the Ford Motor Company. He had also penned winning Formula 1 machinery as well. He was one of the world's most talented, and underappreciated, architects of racing machinery. The fact that today, 35 years later, the Spec Racer he designed remains the most popular, and most successful, racing car in the world, speaks volumes for his talent.

The car features a robust steel tube frame chassis, with open cockpit fiberglass body. It has a mid-engine, mated to a five speed transmission. It has disc brakes on all four wheels, with independent suspension on each corner. It has proved over the decades to be reliable, fast, fun, and safe. To date, despite being the most raced car in the world, there has never been a fatality in this car.

When we came onto this scene in the mid-nineties the class was going through its first major upgrade. The Spec Racer Renault had been a phenomenal success. When it was first introduce, the price for a kit to build one of the cars was only about $6,000. In almost no time over 750 of the cars had been sold. This number of race cars being produced was unheard of. But, after ten years it had become time for an upgrade- primarily, because, despite the success of its race car, Renault had not been successful in the US car market. Its subsequent exit led to a shortage of replacement parts and engines for the racer. Therefore, SCCA had partnered with the Ford Motor Company to create an upgrade kit for the cars. This new package included a larger 1.9 liter 4 cylinder engine, versus the original 1.3 liter Renault. It also came with a new 5 speed transmission, and larger brakes. The result was a heavier, but much faster machine. It was clear to all concerned that the future of the class required that they be converted into this new Ford-based configuration. Most Spec Renault racers understood, and embraced, the need for the conversion. A few, however, for whatever reasons, chose to sell their cars rather than go through the expense and effort of making the conversions. In my memory, the cost of the conversion kits were about $6,000- roughly the same as the original cost of the cars a decade earlier. Consequently, there were a number of unconverted, reasonably priced cars for sale at the time that we decided to get back into racing. Mike and Mark, with my encouragement, purchased the car that was for sale in Georgia.

Approximately, a year later, Sherry and I purchased another Spec Renault- from a different guy in Georgia. We also ordered a new race trailer- sized to accommodate two spec racers. My recollection is that we also ordered two conversion kits for the cars. Mike had agreed to perform the conversions in his garage- God Bless His Soul!

I remember racing the car in its Spec Renault configuration one time- at Homestead. The impressions I carry with me were that the car was light and very responsive to drive. Shifting its transmission very much of the "stirring about and hoping to find the right gear" variety. It was a lot of fun, but it was also slow. I recall racing in that event against another Renault that was driven by a fellow by the name of Ron Inge. He was slightly faster than me. Shortly after that outing he converted his car, and we converted ours. With that there were no more Spec Renaults racing in Florida.

Chapter Twenty Seven: The Spec Ford Years

The converted cars, now known as Spec Racer Fords, were heavier, less "tossable" to drive, but also faster- on some tracks, four or five seconds a lap faster. The racing that resulted was great. Fields were packed- it was not unusual to have 40 or more cars on some grids. And, for some of the bigger national races it was not unheard of to have almost ninety cars on the track. Over the years a ton of guys raced these cars.

We raced them as we could. Our initial plan had been to try to rent out a seat in one of our cars, while we took turns driving the other car. But, I don't remember us ever succeeding in doing that. Honestly, it was a poorly conceived plan. There was too much competition (re, RMS), and besides, it was just too much fun to drive ourselves. Mike at this time was single, and able to keep the cars in the garage of his Cutler Ridge townhome. He also had plenty of time to tinker on them. We raced when we could – 2 to 3 times a year. It was fun.

Our real lives, of course, continued to change. Sherry and I were in Atlanta for six years before I had an opportunity to relocate to Birmingham, Alabama with a different company. It was a big move for us. I also seem to recall that Mark had remarried, and shortly after that had moved out of state. But, at least we still had racing. We would fly down occasionally, meet Mike at one track or another, and go racing. It was always fun. Rarely was I ever competitive- definitely a mid-field guy. Mike was usually quicker. It was a great time. Eventually, Mike's life took a different turn as well. He fell in love with a delightful young lady by the name of Sandra- a beautiful Venezuelan. It wasn't long before they were married. And, then they had a chance to relocate to Chicago where Mike had been offered a tremendous work-related opportunity. They, of course, took advantage of the opportunity and moved.

This, obviously, created a challenge for our racing together. Mike generously offered to continue to prep the cars in Chicago so that we could race together in that area. That could have worked, but honestly, neither Sherry nor I were all that keen about flying north to race. Our homes, and families, and the tracks that we loved were in the South, and especially in Florida. Therefore, we decided that we finally needed to split Caribbean Motorsports up. It was a tough thing to have to do.

We were together at Sebring. I told Mike about my decision after our final race that weekend. It was a tearful time- in some ways almost like a divorce- but, also a lot better. I think we all knew that it was the right thing to do. It was time. I told Mike to keep the trailer and his car. Then, we ceremoniously pushed my car over to the tent of Robinson Motor Sports. It seemed almost like a symbolic dissolution of CMS- after more than a decade of working, racing, and laughing together. We all shed some tears that afternoon. I remember going back to the hotel after that and pouring myself a very stiff Scotch. Actually, I think I poured several!

For the next ten years we raced with Mick Robinson and Robinson Motor Sports. With his team we always knew that the cars would be well prepared, well set up, safe, and competitive. He provided a true "arrive and drive" experience. All I had to do was call him, tell him at which event we wanted to next race, and show up. Oh, and also, write the check to pay him for the services he provided. Fortunately, at this time my career allowed me to do that. With RMS we frequently raced at Sebring, Daytona, Homestead and Moroso. But, we also occasionally ran at Road Atlanta, and at Barber Motorsports Park in Birmingham. Sherry and I both have great memories of the better part of a decade that we spent racing with Mick and his associates.

Even if my memory allowed (which it most certainly doesn't) it would be far too difficult to attempt to document all the multitude of races run during this period- probably close to fifty. But, throughout the entire period I had the greatest respect for Mick and his company. Never did anything occur that caused me to question in the least Mick's professionalism, integrity, honesty, and love for racing. He always provided a first class, but fairly priced service. Most importantly, when I arrived to race I always knew that my car would be ready, and safe.

One of the most enjoyable aspects of racing with RMS was interacting with his company's various employees, and racing against, and getting to know, his other clients. Four of Mick's long-time employees stand out in my memory- Mark Eaton, Hector De La Torriente, A.J. Hulse, and Dabney Smith. They all have my respect, and deserve a great deal of thanks for the help they each provided me over the years.

To end this section I want to highlight three different episodes with the team that standout in my memory.

The first took place before I even officially transferred my car to RMS. At that time there was an annual 12-hour race put on by SCCA's South Florida Region. Essentially, almost all of the closed-wheel cars that competed in the Club were eligible to enter the race- as long as they had functioning headlights. Fortunately, the rules allowed the installation of temporary removable lights on the Spec Racers. I had always loved and preferred endurance racing- see our IMSA background. Therefore, I badly wanted to do this race in a Spec.

But, before I get to this story, I will take a detour to provide a little bit of background. I actually already had experience with this particular event. In 1993, following the end of the IMSA season, Caribbean Motorsports had entered one of our Preludes in an earlier version of this race for Mike, Mark, and I to drive. This edition of this race was held at Moroso (now known as Palm Beach Motorsports Park)- a track outside of West Palm Beach. In this race, we had done exceptionally well- we eventually finished second overall, and first in class. The only car that had finished in front was a much faster Mosler Consulier- essentially, a mid-engine, road going missile of a car. One item of note for this race is that, towards the conclusion of it, we made the totally illegal, and somewhat illogical, decision to let the licensed, but non-entered, John Schunzel, our team's loyal gas man, have a stint behind the wheel. We were so far ahead at that time that we weren't concerned about where we would finish, and we badly wanted to reward John for all he'd done for the team over the years. I cautioned John, as forcefully as I could, that he must not wreck the car, and in particular, he needed to take care when going through the fast esses in the last section of the track. I advised him to always go into that corner a little slower than it seemed he could, and to never, ever, once he was committed to that corner, lift the throttle. I knew that trailing throttle over-steer was the surest way to spin off the track, crash, and possibly end up in the swamp. John, to his credit, did a fine job. He didn't spin, crash or do anything to call attention to himself. And, his times were actually respectable. Today, I'm not particularly proud that we broke the rules, but I am very glad that we were able to give John this experience.

Speaking of running at Moroso, and the possibility of ending up in the swamp, brings to mind three separate events there that involved our team. The first involved Sherry, and Lance Stewart. For some reason we had brought a Prelude to Moroso for an open track day. This event was sponsored, I believe by the Palm Beach Driving Club, and for a fee anyone could drive around the track. There were race cars running, as well as pure street cars. In particular, I recall that some fellows had even rented a Ford Thunderbird for the day from Hertz. By the end of the afternoon that car had burned up all of its brakes, and the engine was smoking heavily. I have no idea of how their return at the Hertz counter ended.

But, what I wanted to mention in particular was an experience that Sherry had in the car. As the day had progressed, and after we'd accomplished whatever we'd been there to accomplish, we talked Lance

Stewart into giving various members of the team rides around the track in the Prelude. I seem to recall that for some reason Chuck Jones from California was there. I think we were still trying to see if he could secure funding for the following season for the team. Towards that end Chuck wanted to ride around the track with Lance- ostensibly so that he could evaluate Lance's driving style and ability. After that Lance offered to take the rest of us for a ride. I remember riding with him, and marveling at what he was able to do with the car. Compared with how I drove his skills were in another dimension. He was able to slide the car in ways that I couldn't even imagine doing- all the while retaining perfect control- with precision. I was amazed.

After my ride Sherry climbed into the passenger seat for her session with Lance. I was delighted that she was going to finally be able to experience what it was like inside of a race car going fast. She'd ridden with me behind the wheel earlier, but I don't think she'd been all that impressed. I knew that a few laps riding with Lance would give her an entirely different experience. They made three or four circuits around the track. I could tell that Lance was enjoying putting on a show for Sherry- he was driving very quickly. I followed the car carefully as it wound around the track. While I had all the confidence in the world in Lance, I still couldn't help but be just a little apprehensive. Then, as they flew down the back stretch and entered the treacherous fast back esses, at a speed well in excess of a hundred and twenty miles per hour, the car immediately in front of them spun. The driver of that car had made the critical mistake of entering the turn too fast, and then lifting off the throttle. When he did that weight had transferred off the rear wheels and the car had instantly spun. I knew that there was very, very little room for Lance to be able to maneuver around a spinning car at that narrow portion of the track. Unfortunately, just as all this occurred the cars disappeared behind a grandstand that stood between the track and where I was standing. I couldn't see what happened from then on. But, I could hear a loud thump as one, or both, of the cars impacted something heavily. I was instantly very concerned. It seemed to take longer than I thought it should have before the Prelude finally emerged from behind the screening grandstand. Fortunately, the car and its passenger were unharmed. When he came into the pits Lance calmly related how he'd anticipated the car ahead spinning, and had therefore been able to avoid the crash. The spinning car, however, had not been so fortunate. It had impacted the earth bank on the left of the track hard. It was essentially destroyed. The track was closed for the rest of the day. Sherry had very much enjoyed her much more than bargained for ride!

A less positive experience at that corner involved another of our drivers from the previous IMSA season. Dan Nye had his sights set on moving up into the ranks of professional motorsports professionals. And, his family had sufficient funding to allow him to pursue this goal. Towards that end he was participating in that winter's Skip Barber Dodge Pro Series, a higher level championship for a faster spec of open wheeled Formula Cars. One weekend's set of races took place at the Moroso track. Unfortunately, Dan was involved in a heavy crash at the track- while going through the fast back esses. He, and his car, somersaulted out of the track, and deep into the swamp. He was badly injured in the crash, suffering severe brain trauma. For many weeks it was questionable if he would survive. He did, but I believe that he was never able to make a full recovery. We felt very bad for Dan. He was a talented, and likeable guy!

Another unfortunate event for the team took place later at this same corner. Mike had brought one of the Preludes up to Moroso at the suggestion of Fran Broadfoot. A friend of Fran's was interested in purchasing the car, and wanted to drive it on the track before agreeing to buy it. This potential buyer had previous racing experience, and supposedly knew what he was doing. But, for whatever reason, he somehow managed to comprehensively destroy the Prelude in the fast esses. Now, we wanted $15,000. Fran advised that, while he thought the guy was good for the money, we should take possession of one of the guy's collector cars as collateral until the guy gave us the money. Fran was a very smart guy. We should have listened. The guy never paid. Jerk!

The back esses at Moroso were one of the most dangerous corners in sports car racing. I was delighted when this section was eliminated when the track was redesigned.

But, enough about Moroso's fast back esses. At this time the Florida Region's 12 Hour event was no longer held at Moroso. Now it was scheduled at the Homestead Motor Speedway. I called Mick Robinson to enquire has to whether he had a seat available for this race. As it turned out, he did. He planned to enter two cars, and would be happy to have me drive in one of them. He anticipated having three drivers in each car- teams would be assigned later. We were on.

We'd actually had previous experience racing a Spec Ford in this event. The prior year CMS had entered one of its cars in the race. For the first half of the race we'd performed well- essentially running third behind two Robinson Motor Sports cars. Then as the sun began to set our guest driver managed to comprehensively blow up the engine. It was an expensive mistake. I didn't want to run my own car in that race again.

As it turned out I was to be teamed in the second RMS car with Hector De La Torriente, an RMS employee; and with Phil Tapia. Phil was a nice guy, and reasonably quick driver. I seem to remember that he did work for ESPN- designing high-tech digital displays, and screens.

Hector had worked with RMS for a number of years. He was a tall Cuban kid. He had learned to race from Mick and Mark Eaton. I had raced against him in the past, and knew that he was quick- if sometimes a just little wild and aggressive. I thought we had a good team.

The other RMS entry was to be piloted by another employee, the very quick Mark Eaton; a fun, but quick, older guy from the Turks and Caicos, named Rodney Thompson; and another quick guy from Florida, Larry Baisden. I knew that this teaming had won the race the previous year. They were, of course, favored to repeat.

Hector started the race in our car. Mark Eaton was in the lead car. They ran nose to tail the entire session. I had already learned that it was a matter of pride for Hector to be able to run with Mark. Over the years of working together they had developed a strong on-track rivalry. At the first round of stops, Rodney Thompson was plugged into the other car, and I climbed aboard our car. For the next hour we also ran essentially nose to tail. I could hear over the in-car radio delight on the part of my team. Clearly, they hadn't expected that I would be able to run with Rodney. After two and a half hours RMS was running a strong first, and second. Then our other team mates had their turns in the car. The same results. The two teams were still tied closely together.

I would like to mention at this time that the catering for the team was provided by Hector's parents- Hector, Sr. (Big Hector), and his wife Maricela- both of whom were great cooks- in a decidedly Cuban style. And, they were also both great people. Over the years we got to know them much better (more on that to come). One of the highlights of the meals and refreshments was the genuine Cuban-style espresso coffee that they made track side in a traditional Cuban pewter pot. A mini-cup, or two, of that and we were good for going another couple of seconds faster on the track. It was memorable stuff. And, none of us had to worry about being alert when the sun went down.

For the first half of the race our car was in great shape- running second, still in close touch with the leading car. All we had to do now was to finish! I should mention now just what a great endurance racing car the Spec Racer Ford is. It was quicker than most other cars on the track- that always helps. It was almost like we were driving a Le Mans-style prototype racer as we sped around, and passed almost everything else on the track. In this race it was common for us to pass four, or more, cars each lap. I don't care what anyone may say- being able to do that when you're racing is fun! The car was also, normally, ultra reliable. Remember, it had been designed by Roy Lunn, one of the world's greatest automotive engineers. He'd learned his early lessons helping to design one of the world's greatest endurance racers- The Ford GT40.

The Spec Racer Ford had very few weak links. The brake pads would easily last for 12 hours, or more. It was also, relatively easy on tires. I don't think we had to change tires in the race, either. All we had to do was periodically put gas in it-a little over six gallons about every hour and fifteen minutes.

When you drive a race car around the same track for such a long period of time you tend to pick up on things that you wouldn't otherwise notice. For example, we had a lap time readout mounted on the dash of the car. I discovered during my first stint that I could monitor on the readout the impact that different lines around the track made on my lap times. Then, in a later stint, as the hot Florida sun began to go down and the track began to cool, I could immediately see my lap times getting better. I very much enjoyed being able to pay attention to these kinds of things as I was driving.

I bragged earlier about the usual reliability of the Spec Racer Ford. But, at that time it did have one weak link- the car's alternator. This unit was the same stock unit used in the passenger cars for which the engine was originally designed- a Ford Escort, if I recall. Cheap, and good enough for street use- but, unfortunately, not up to dealing with the heat, vibrations, and strain of working for hours on end in an endurance racing car. Just when everything seemed to be going our way, towards the end of my second stint in the car, this piece of equipment gave up. One minute everything was perfect. The next, coming onto the front stretch (just *past* the entrance into the pits) I heard the engine give an unusual popping sound- almost like the engine had back fired. Then, as I attempted to accelerate out of the second corner the engine totally died. The powerless car and I ended up stranded on the outside of the third corner- across the track from any corner workers that might have been able to quickly assist us in getting the car back to the garage. Being stranded where I was, on the outside of the track, there was no way that I could be reached by a tow vehicle until the race was brought under control with a full course caution. It seemed to take forever before this was made to happen. While I waited we lost several laps to the leader. Finally, a rescue truck reached me, and began towing the car, with me still in the cockpit, back to the garage. As this slowly took place, we lost even more laps. Then, once the car was in the pits, the team began the task of changing the alternator. Of course, the crew had already diagnosed the likely issue after conversations with me over the in-car radio. Making this simple repair only took them a few minutes- they'd had lots of practice. But, when the car rejoined the race, because of the time it had taken for the car to be towed back, we were many, many laps down. There was still over six hours left to run in the race- but, now some of the fun was out of it. Of course, it's never exactly drudgery being able to drive a race car around a track. It is still fun. But, when you're no longer trying to win the race, some of the excitement is missing. But, regardless, I can still remember just how pleasurable it was driving the track at night. The team had installed high powered driving lights on a bracket that quickly snapped onto the pins that held the bodywork in place. As soon as it got dark all they had to do was to pin the bracket in place, and plug a single pigtail into a socket that had been installed to provide power.

Driving a racing car at speed in the darkness is a unique experience. Initially, it takes a lap or two to become fully reoriented. But, surprisingly quickly you adapt. In fact, I always found that it was, in some ways, easier to drive at night- it was easier then to focus on only the things upon which you needed to focus. Easier that is, if you were one of the fastest cars on the track. But, if you were in a slower car constantly being passed, for me that was not the case. In that situation you are not so much worried about driving as you are about not getting in the way of the cars passing you. The problem is that you don't really know who's coming up behind you- the dazzling glare from the brilliant driving lights of the cars behind you tends to be very distracting. The worst example I ever experienced of this was in a Firestone Firehawk race at Sebring. The car I was driving was in the Touring class- the slowest of the three classes in the race. It was a pitch black night on a dark track. The race was under a full course caution, and for some reason I had ended up towards the head of the field. Then, after the race went green, it was totally impossible to tell if the car inches from my bumper was a much faster car, or was a competitor racing with me. Eventually, after just a few corners, I understood that all I could do was quit worrying about what was going on behind me, and focus instead on driving my own race. I learned to let whoever was behind me find their own way past. But, that wasn't a problem for me at Homestead- I was in one of the quickest cars. It was, simply, a joy to drive the car at night. As the sun had gone down the temperature had fallen. Now, the heat in the open cockpit car- from the engine, radiator, and brake- was offset by the cool air rushing past. I could easily have driven that car all night. But, of course, the schedule for refueling wouldn't allow that. Eventually, I had to pit and hand the car over to my "chomping at the bit" team mate. He finished the race- I think we may have ended up in the top ten- but, we were still laps down to our team car which eventually won the race after a battle with a strong Porsche 911. I discovered that day that I loved driving the Spec Racer Ford in endurance races.

The second adventure with Mick that I'd like to document involved him helping to improve my driving through the use of a data system. When I'd first begun racing there was no such thing as data capture on a racing car. It was all seat of the pants stuff. But, in the 1990's, this technology had appeared in high level racing- but, at that time, it was difficult and extremely expensive to use. But, by the early 2000's these systems had made its way into club racing.

Essentially, what these systems do is to digitally record information from various electronic sensors placed on the car. This captured data can then be reviewed- usually with the help of software loaded onto a lap top computer. The number of sensors that can be recorded is limited only by the size of the in-car computer, and by the ability of the user to understand what the data is telling them.

After several years of watching some of the fastest guys in the class use this approach I finally gave in and asked Mick to install a system on my car. The program that Mick utilized was from "CDS." I seem to recall that the cost of the complete system was about four thousand dollars. In my racing budget that was a lot of money- but, honestly, I found that it was money extremely well spent. In retrospect, I wish that I had done it years' earlier.

Some of the key variables that we chose to record were time, speed, g-force loading, throttle position, brake pressure, gearing, and engine RPMs. In addition, the system had GPS capability which allowed the system to produce a map of the track. The software then layered the recorded data onto this track map. Doing this allowed the analysis of speed, time, and all other aspects of performance on every inch of the track's surface, on every lap. Now we could really see what was taking place on the track.

It didn't take long for me to recognize that "Data don't lie!" Now, everyone could know if you were really taking a given corner flat like you'd said, or if instead you were actually cracking the throttle imperceptibly to provide yourself a margin of comfort. But with data, there was no place that the driver could hide. I absolutely loved having this information, and I loved working with Mick (for a fee) to improve my skills.

The very first time we reviewed data from my car he could immediately see two things that I had been doing wrong on the track- two simple things, that when corrected, dropped my lap times by over a second. The first was the speed at which I was shifting gears. Data showed that I was being too careful, and too slow, with my shifts. The other, more significant, problem was in how I was applying the brakes. Again, I was being too careful, trying to be smooth. As a result I was gently easing onto the brakes before beginning to apply significant pressure on the pedal. I was using the brakes like we all do when driving on the street.

Despite really knowing that Mick was probably correct, I began to defend my usual technique, saying that I tried to be gentle so that my front tires wouldn't lock up. Mick patiently explained that using this new technique they couldn't slide since, under hard braking, so much weight was transferred to the front tires. Consequently, they were able to do much more work than under normal circumstances. As he told me this I remembered what I learned about this at Skippy School, and the formula that they'd drilled into us that showed that the amount of work a tire could do was a function of its coefficient of friction times the amount of weight placed on it.

As I thought about what Mick had shared this all made so much sense. I was anxious to put these new techniques into practice. The next time out in the car, because of these changes, I was able to immediately shave a second off my lap times. I was impressed, and anxious to find other ways to shave time from my laps.

Over time, I learned that the best way to use data is to compare your data from a session of a given track against the data from a faster driver, in the same type of car, on that track. That can be done either by downloading shared data, or by actually putting the faster driver in your car. Either way you end up with two sets of data that can be compared.

One of the first places to start when making such comparisons is to review the points where the drivers initiate braking for each corner. The system we were using clearly showed where that was on the track, exactly measured down to the foot. In general, Mick's data showed that, on most corners, he applied the brakes at the same spots as I did- maybe even a little earlier- with just a couple of exceptions. The most glaring difference was at the entrance to Turn 17- the last corner at Sebring- a corner that had always intimidated me slightly. This turn is at the end of the long back straight- our cars were doing 130 mph at the entrance to the corner. This corner is complex, and, despite eventually requiring a total direction change of 180 degrees, is quite fast. The first part of the turn is actually taken flat- no brakes, and no lifting off the accelerator- until a point just before where the second part of the corner begins. Once that unmarked spot is reached hard threshold braking is required, along with downshifting two gears. Then, once you have slowed the car sufficiently to allow you to rotate the car into the corner, power must immediately be reapplied- going to, and holding, full power absolutely as soon as possible. Mick's data showed some glaring differences with how I was doing the corner. He was braking twenty feet deeper for this corner, and he was going back to the power earlier, and harder. Again, I was being too gentle, and too careful. As we discussed this corner I told Mick that I was amazed that he could accelerate as early, and as hard. Clearly, doing this allowed him to have significantly more exit speed than I did. He laughed, and told me that I simply had to understand that, given what the data shows, the car can take it. Trust me, "you'll give up before the car will!" Since then I've tried to remember that every time I have driven that corner. Eventually, my times through this corner became very close to his. Again, money and time well spent.

Turn One at Sebring is one of the most challenging corners on the track. It is a fast left hander- in our cars the turn is taken in excess of ninety miles per hour, if done correctly. One of the things that makes this corner so difficult is that the apex of the corner, and the turn's track out point, is blind when you enter the corner- they are hidden behind the tall concrete guard rail that lines the inside of the track. Granted, there is usually a cone sitting on top of the fence to mark the apex point. But, still- its takes real commitment to steer a car into a 90 mph bend, and then go to full power, without actually being able to see where you are going! There is always just a little temptation to brake a little too hard, or to wait a little too long, before getting fully back to power. Just a comfort thing- you know? But, doing these things right will immediately separate you from the guys ahead. If you want to be fast you can't allow yourself the luxury of this kind of comfort.

This was the corner that Mick and I concentrated on next. Generally, the most time on any track can be found in fast corners that lead onto long straights. As we reviewed the data we could see that while we were braking at about the same spot- but, I was slowing a little too much, and going back to full power just a slightly later. How much later? Only by about ten feet. On the data map it was easy to see where we both accelerated- down to the foot. How much difference in time were these differences causing? Not much, about a tenth of a second. Now, a tenth of a second doesn't sound like much, but I understood that, with seventeen turns at Sebring, these kinds of differences could quickly add up.

One of the most valuable things that Mick and I did, after my lap times had started to improve, was to overlay our sector times. The system broke the lap around the track into segments- each corner, and each straight between those corners. It could even break each corner into multiple segments- entry, mid-corner, and exit. I badly wanted to know exactly where on the track I was losing time to Mick. Was I slower through the hairpin? Was I not as quick through Turn 17? I was hoping, of course, that there was just one sector that I needed to focus on? But, unfortunately, that is not what the data showed. This analysis showed that, after we'd made the easy improvements to my technique, I was losing about a tenth of a second in each corner. Then, when we broke down the corner segments further, we could see that the time differences were consistently attributable to over-slowing, and to a slight delay in going to power to accelerate out of each corner. As I thought about this I came to think of it as my "a risk reduction factor." In other words, it was simply in my nature, as a banker, to limit the risk I was incurring until I felt certain that it was at an acceptable level. I learned that that was a tough habit to change. To do so meant changing, fundamentally, a part of who I was. Consequently, those were very tough tenths to find. Eventually, I got my times down within a couple of seconds, on the long Sebring track, to the pole sitters. But, improving my times any further had gotten increasingly more difficult. The first seconds are relatively easy to find. But, after that, each further improvement becomes increasingly more difficult to find. Time for a racer is a very tough mistress.

Another great thing about racing with Mick was the opportunity it presented to get to know better the folks that you are racing against. It was common for Mick to have six or more cars under "his tent." At the track, especially when you are in an "arrive and drive" arrangement, there is a usually lots of down time for the driver. In other words, there was time for us drivers to get to know each other, and their families. When Mike and I were racing together we really didn't have these opportunities. We were, of course, the only ones under our "tent." And, equally important, our arrangement was definitely not of the "arrive and drive" variety. We had to do everything ourselves. If the tires or brakes needed to be changed, we had to do it. It the car needed fuel, we had to do it. If the car needed to be cleaned, we had to do it. It was still easier than when we were racing professionally, but because we were usually busy we never really got to know many other drivers. But, racing with Mick, was different. Not only did we get to know the drivers on his team. But, since Mick provided parts, and advice, for all the other racers at the track we got to know many of them as well. Sherry and I enjoyed this aspect of racing with Mick very much. We had a lot of good times, and made a lot of good friends, sitting and chatting under Mick's big tent.

For the most part the folks who raced with Mick were pleasant, and honorable, folks who got along well together. Generally, we even managed to keep any on-track squabbles to nothing more than friendly, respectable disagreements. That was not always possible, of course, but usually, Mick and his guys, were alert to any issues that might need to be dealt with back at the tent. He was good at calming the waters- both because of his nature, and because, since he was so experienced, he was immensely respected by all the racers. Mick had been a key player in the Spec Racer series since its very inception- having won multiple championships.

Some of the on-track action- altercations that had the potential to be acrimonious- actually ended up, because of the camaraderie under the tent, being humorous. In that respect, I remember one test day at Sebring, in particular. I believe this session was the last one scheduled for the day. I remember that the temperature was pleasant. It already had been a long test day. We'd all had more than enough time to work on whatever we felt that we needed to work on. Because of that, there was no real pressure on any of us to set a quick time. All our tires were nearly worn out anyway. We were all on the track just to have fun. So, there we were, four or five of the guys who raced under Mick's tent, speeding tightly together down the track's back straight, heading towards the difficult, and fast, Turn Seventeen. I remember that when we reached that corner we were, at least, three wide- fortunately, I was on the inside. Then, we all turned in together. Of course, none of us wanted to be out-braved. I knew, as we went into the turn, that it was tight. But, I was on the inside- and there was no way that I was going to give up to anyone. Besides, I knew that the guys on the outside would eventually have to give way as we went through the corner. I remember concluding that, unbelievably, we were probably going to get through the corner without incident. Then, I felt the slightest tap on the right rear of my car. The guy behind me, Rodney Thompson, had, apparently, decided that it would be a lot more fun if he made it **four** wide into the corner! Of course, as soon as he touched my car it spun. Then, his car spun. In fact, all of the cars entering the corner eventually spun! Essentially, what had happened was that all of the cars operating under Mick's tent were spinning together, simultaneously, at the fastest corner on the track. It could have, perhaps should have, easily turned into a huge mess. But, instead we all got through it undamaged. When we got back to the tent, I remember that we all got out of our cars, and started to look accusingly at each other. But, then, Rodney Thompson just grinned. And, with that, rather than anyone being angry, we all broke out laughing.

Rodney was one of the fellows that I most enjoyed racing against. He was about my same age- older than many of the folks that we raced against. Like me, he'd been racing for ages. We both knew what was what. But, what I liked best about Rodney was his sense of humor. Beneath his gruff demeanor there was always fun looking for an opportunity to escape. I remember too that he was constantly aware of what was going on around him, and if someone ever did anything peculiar, Rodney would always pick up on it. He was, of course, too much of a gentleman to actually comment, not wanting to cause any embarrassment. But, you could see in his eyes what he was thinking. We frequently exchanged knowing winks and nods about what had just occurred.

Over the years I had concluded that, in earlier life, Rodney had probably been either a Caribbean pirate, or a merchant who did business with these "Brethren of the Coast." There was just an aura about him, and the way he handled himself, that led one to reach that conclusion. And, in real life, he actually wasn't too far removed from that sort of life. He ran the largest (and, perhaps, only) air freight business operating into, and out, of the Turks and Caicos. At some point, as I researched pirates in the Bahamas, I learned that there was actually a fellow named Thompson, at the time the most prominent merchant in the Abacos, who specialized in fencing property for the area's pirates. I always wanted to question Rodney if they were related. But, I never did. Rodney and I were good friends.

But, not all on track skirmishes ended as amicably as the episode I described earlier. There was a guy (who shall remain nameless) that raced out of Ft. Myers. He and I were about the same age, and, on the track, we were usually about the same speed. For a couple of seasons we seemed to end up frequently racing against each other. Generally, we got along well. I even considered him to be a friend. But, then I felt that he intentionally put me in a position that, theoretically, could have killed me. Needless to say, I wasn't happy about that- not in the least.

We were racing the Long Course at Sebring. Going into the Hairpin corner we were racing closely- I knew that he was probably going to try to pass me under braking. He'd thought about trying it the previous lap. But, I also knew that, if he wasn't alongside before we began to brake, he wouldn't be able to pull such a pass off. Over the years I'd learned that I can brake for that corner- while still retaining control- as late as anyone. Consequently, I knew that since he wasn't yet beside me, that if I went to my normal braking point before applying the brakes, he would not be able to successfully pass. I knew that if he tried to pass by delaying his braking until after I did, he would then just lock his tires, and slide wide when he needed to turn into the corner. As I had expected, that's exactly what he attempted to do. It was just a rookie move. Knowing what was going to happen, I gave him plenty of room, and then calmly turned safely under him. I thought it was a classic move on my part.

But, apparently, being outsmarted like this really got the guy's dander up. This is more commonly referred to in racing as experiencing "Red Mist!" In other words, a description of the color commonly said to descend over a driver's eyes when he loses his temper. He had actually carried so much speed into the corner, and through the grass on the outside of the corner that we emerged at the exit to the turn side by side. The run from the second gear hairpin to the right handed Cunningham Corner is a distance of close to third of a mile. In between these turns is a set of sweeping right, and then left, bends. We went into the first of these fast turns side by side. These corners are easily taken flat out in fourth gear- at roughly one hundred miles per hour. These sweeps are so wide, and so easy, that normally there is plenty of room for two cars, maybe even three cars, to easily go through them side by side. And, I knew, that since I was on the inside of the track, that when we finally got to the upcoming Cunningham turn I would easily be able to pass him going into that bend. But, I think this guy may have figured this out, too. That's the only reason I've ever been able to come up with why he decided to run me off the track through these sweeps. At the point where he should have been on the left side of the track I suddenly found him pushing up against the left side of my car- attempting to shove me off the track at one hundred miles per hour. At that point, I had no choice but to back off. If I hadn't, I'd have crashed.

After the race, I confronted him about what he'd done. I even showed him the tire rub marks he'd left on the side of my car- clear evidence of the impact. He tried to stammer out a denial that he'd even known he'd been near me. Fortunately, at that point, before I had decided whether or not to hit him, I realized that his teenage daughter was standing nearby and watching with an open mouth. With that realization, I turned, and walked away. I certainly didn't want to embarrass him in front of his kid. But, I have never forgotten what he'd tried to do to me. As far as I know, he never came to a race again. Certainly, not a race in which I was entered.

The last episode of racing with Mick Robinson that I'd like to share again involved Hector De La Torriente. By this time Hector was actually dating Sherry's daughter, my step-daughter, Anna. We'd introduced them at a race at Sebring. It was clear that they, shall we say, very much enjoyed each other's company. (They later married, and have given us two wonderful grandchildren!) But, this particular race was at Birmingham's Barber Motorsports Park. It was a very well attended SCCA Regional Race.

For the feature race I was gridded somewhere about tenth. Hector, was near the front- maybe third. The weather for the weekend had been atrocious. For the race, it was raining- heavily. The Barber facility if one of the best, and most beautiful, in the entire country. It was built by George Barber- and, was conceived as the "Augusta National" of race tracks. The perimeter and surrounds of the track are beautifully landscaped and feature many whimsical and/or thought-provoking bronze sculptures. The track itself features many fast blind corners that bend up and down over the rolling Alabama countryside. It's a fun place to race.

But, this race was run in the rain. And, as the race continued, the rain increased in intensity. It wasn't long before the sides of the course were littered with cars that had slid off into the gravel traps and gotten stuck. At one point in particular, just after the high speed chicane, a number of cars had gone off- separately. But, they had all ended up stuck alongside each other. I knew that the first one that had gone off had been the pole sitter. Another one had started a few cars ahead of me. By the time the race had ended, Hector had won, and I was in fifth! We were both extremely pleased with our results. The family dined together that night over some very good steaks. I also seem to recall sharing a bottle of Champagne at some point during the evening. A good time.

Book Four: Dies Irae- Ingemisco

"But, Thou, Oh Good One, Show Mercy

Lest I Burn in Everlasting Fire,

Give Me a Place Among the Sheep,

And Separate Me From the Goats…"

Chapter Twenty Eight: Cuban American Racing

I retired from being productively employed in 2012, at age 64. Compass Bank, the Birmingham, Alabama-based bank that I had spent the previous 12 years working for, had been acquired two years earlier by Banco Balboa Viscaya Argentaria, a Spanish banking company, more commonly referred to as BBVA. I spent those two years assisting BBVA, to the best of my ability, with its assimilation of the new acquisition. But, at the end of that period it was time for them to install their own people, and time for me to move on. I didn't mind. I was ready to get on with the next phase of my life.

Retirement brings many changes to your life. And, one of the changes that I knew that I'd have to make was to give up "Arrive and Drive" racing. Without a large salary, and frequent bonuses, there was no way that I could continue to pay someone to provide this service for me. But, I wasn't quite ready to stop racing. Fortunately, I didn't have to.

My step-daughter Anna, and racing mechanic/co-driver Hector De La Torriente, had decided to marry a number of years earlier. We'd been delighted when we'd learned that they'd decided to "tie the knot." And, not just because that Hector had proposed to Anna on top of a motor home overlooking Turn 15 during the Sebring 12 Hour! Rather, we were delighted because we knew that they would make a good couple, and were very deeply in love. That much had been obvious from the instant that we introduced them to each other at Sebring several years earlier.

The occasion had been Sherry's 50th birthday. To mark that occasion we'd invited all of our five children to come to the Sebring racetrack at which I was scheduled to race in a SCCA Regional event. (Okay- I know that it sounds a little strange to celebrate your wife's 50th birthday at a race track, but..... I guess that's kind of what this book is about.)

Anyway, we introduced our kids to all the Robinson Motor Sports crew-just to be polite. But, after Anna and Hector had met it was obvious that there was chemistry between them. Normally, at the track Hector was always attentive to the drivers as they sat in their cars, buckled in- waiting to be waved onto the track. But, I very distinctly remember for that afternoon's race being surprised when Hector hadn't come by to check, as I sat in the car, whether I needed anything. This was so unusual that I looked around to see where he was, and much to my surprise, and delight, I could see that he and Anna were sitting nearby in the Team golf cart-just happily chatting away. I told Sherry that night that when I saw this I knew that something was going to happen between them- it took a lot to take Hector's mind off of racing!

As retirement neared, Hector and I had several conversations about whether I was going to continue racing. I assured him that I would not be able to continue doing what I'd done for the last decade. By this time, Hector was no longer working with Robinson Motor Sports. He'd left Mick's company not long after he'd met Anna to take advantage of an opportunity to work with a race team in Ormond Beach, Florida that, at that time, prepared and raced Porsches in IMSA. It was a good move for him in a number of respects- one of which was that a few years later Mick decided to sell his company and retire.

I told Hector that I'd be interested in racing my Spec Racer in some endurance races- I'd always been partial to this kind of racing. A few years before SCCA's Central Florida Region and Florida Region had agreed to jointly sponsor an endurance racing series for SCCA eligible cars. This series was known as the Tropical Endurance Series, or TES. It consisted of eight to ten races split between the tracks in each region (CFR:

Daytona and Sebring; FR: Homestead and Moroso). Most of the races were one and a half hour events, with the possibility of there being a few longer races. It sounded perfect to me. Hector and I could run together in these races. I would provide the financial backing, and Hector agreed to prep the car. The name of our team- in honor of Hector's heritage-would be Cuban American Racing! Or, "CAR" for short.

Initially, we planned to run only a few races a year- just for fun. I purchased an inexpensive, open-wheeled trailer, and we were in business. The first season was definitely a learning season for us. We only ran a few races to see how we'd enjoy this discipline. Unsurprisingly, we loved it. At the end of the year we made a decision to up our game. We wanted to go after the TES Championship the following season.

We did most of the races that year. It took us a while to win a race, but we quickly scored a lot of points. In particular, I remember racing at Daytona that year. Going into the final lap we were running fourth. Hector was driving the car. He loved driving Daytona- he had won at that track multiple times when he'd raced with Mick. He especially loved the nickname that he'd earned there: "Daytona Dominator!" On that last lap one of the cars in front of us ran out of fuel, elevating us to third. But, when we went to post race tech we learned that the leading car had been disqualified for having made too short of a pit stop. Therefore, we were moved up to second. It wasn't a win- but, it was the highest position yet for Cuban American Racing. We were excited.

Our usual team tactics were that I would start the race, then, when we were within the pit window for fuel, I would bring the car in and hand it over to Hector. The series required that any pit stops in which fuel was added must last a minimum of five minutes. The car would actually run 70 minutes on a full tank of fuel. Therefore, in theory, in a normal ninety minute race I could pit after having only been in the car for as little as 15 minutes. I think we only used this extreme tactic one time- at Daytona when we were faced with an extremely strong field of competitors. Since Hector was as fast, or faster, than anyone there, I wanted him to be in the car as long as possible. But, usually, I would drive at least 30 minutes, leaving Hector 55 minutes to drive the car. In races where the competition was not strong I might even drive 45 minutes, leaving Hector to finish the remaining forty minutes. Soon, as we got our act together, and as my driving improved, we began to win races. I think our first victory may have been at Moroso that year. Or, at Sebring, truthfully, I can no longer remember. I do remember, however, that we did win that year's Championship- fulfilling the goal that we'd set for ourselves.

One thing that had become clear as the year went on, was that I'd made a mistake buying an open trailer. I think this became crystal clear after Sherry and I pulled the rig down to Homestead for one of the races towards the end of the season. The trailer pulled great, but since it was open there were limited ways to secure the team's tools and equipment. To support the car in an endurance-race required a significant amount of equipment- stuff like jacks, tools, gas cans, jack stands, chairs, tents, etc. On that trip we resorted to stuffing our valuable equipment into the cab of the pickup- just to ensure that it could be safely locked away. But, we knew that this wasn't practical for Hector and Anna, given their young kids that understandably had priority over the back seat space. Therefore, when we returned from that race I contracted a dealer in the Daytona Beach area to trade the open wheel trailer, and to order a beautiful, new 20 foot, all-aluminum, ATC trailer- specifically equipped to carry a Spec Racer Ford. We had installed two folding aluminum racks that each held four tires and wheels. We also installed "e-trac" rails along the floor, on each side, and across the front walls- using this system we could easily strap down, not only the car, but all of our team equipment, as well. In addition, we mounted several other trick aluminum pieces in the trailer-a dual bay helmet and suit rack, a rack to secure four gas cans, a rack for the floor jack, a shelving system that mounted on the trailer's door, and several other slick add-on pieces. By the time we were ready to go racing we had a very nice package. For the outside of the trailer I had designed large, colorful, custom Cuban American Racing decals, which looked absolutely great. We had also invested in a supply of Cuban American Racing crew shirts. When we showed up for the next season's first race- we looked spiffy- both off the track, and on.

The race car's primary surfaces were painted gloss black, while the minor surfaces were done in bright red. In addition, we'd acquired custom vinyl decal sets for the car's sides and front wheel arches. These decal designs were bright golden flames. The Cuban American Racing machine, in my opinion, was easily the best looking car on the track. We felt good about what we'd put together. Now, the series' defending champions were ready to go racing- again.

Just how ready was documented by us winning *every* race in the Series. We were undefeated in our class. Granted, our competition was not all that strong. But, we won at Moroso; we won at Daytona; we won at Sebring; and we won at Homestead. Not only did we win that year's TES championship, but we also won the SCCA's Southeastern Division's ECR Championship. In the vernacular, we "stunk it up!" Everyone was getting tired of us winning. A couple of memories about that season stand out.

The first race was at Moroso. As usual, I started the race. Hector had qualified the car on the pole. As the flag went down I got a good start, and led going into the first turn. I then continued to lead for several additional laps. But, as those first laps unfolded I realized that I was having some difficulty breathing, and I was a little uncomfortable. I tried to stretch, and made sure that the belts weren't too tight. They were okay. I tried to slow my breathing down, and consciously took deeper breaths. Initially, I thought that I was just hyped up about being in the lead. But, none of the things that I tried to calm down helped, and eventually I realized that was having some kind of medical event. But, I didn't think that I was dying- I was just uncomfortable, and having difficulty breathing. And, besides, my options at that point, were limited because we weren't yet in our pit window. The last thing I wanted to do was jeopardize winning the season's first race. I knew that if I stopped early we would have to make two 5-minute pit stops. We'd never win if I did that. Besides, I was actually leading the race! I think this was maybe the first time that I'd been able to do that on my own. I didn't want to get out of the car. I even remember thinking that there could be worse ways to die than croaking while leading a race!

Before the race I'd told Hector that I'd like to drive 30 minutes- we'd agreed to that plan. And, besides, I knew that I'd need to do at least 20 minutes to be comfortably inside the window for fuel. As the race went on I told Hector over the radio that I wasn't feeling well, and that I would like to get out of the car as soon as we were made 20 minutes. I pitted at that point. He got in the car, and went on to win the race. I stayed in the pits, manned the radio, and talked him through the race. But, I was still not feeling well.

After the checker, Hector and his dad took the car to Victory Lane, but I stayed in the trailer. I took my driving suit off, and tried everything that I could to cool down. I was still hoping that maybe I'd just gotten over heated in the car. Eventually, my breathing did start to become more normal, and, in general, I gradually began to feel better. I think that after a while I even managed to start loading equipment into the trailer. But, still, I knew that I wasn't right. I suspected that I could have suffered some type of mild cardiac event. I thought briefly about reporting to the SCCA medical car, and let the track's medical team evaluate me. But, honestly, I was worried that if I did that they'd certainly put me in an ambulance and take me off to the local hospital. I didn't want to go through that, and I didn't want Hector to have to be delayed, hours away from home, while that happened. I knew that he needed to go to work the next day. That probably wasn't the smartest decision that I've ever made, but I reasoned that I would likely be okay. And, I was. But, all the way home I continued to feel like something wasn't quite right. I only experienced minor chest discomfort, but my breathing was not quite normal, and I felt tired. Three hours later we got back to Ormond, cleaned up, and had dinner. I then told Sherry that I was tired, and needed to go to bed. She knew that was out of character for me. After a victory I usually would have celebrated with several glasses of good scotch, while Hector and I watched in-car videos and relived the day's events. The next morning, as we drove home, I told her what had happened. We agreed that I needed to get to the doctor. Fortunately, after I called her office and explained what had happened, my Internist, Dr. Tracy Vo, urged that I should come right in. She checked me out, concluded that I was stable, but then arranged for me to see a Cardiologist, Dr. Longobardi, the next morning. When we arrived at his office he had his nurse administer an electrocardiogram. Minutes later he reported to us that I'd had a heart attack. I remember he even said that I could have died. He wanted me admitted to the hospital for further evaluation. He suspected that I had blockage in my heart, and, consequently, was still at some risk. The next morning I was on my way to heart surgery- one of the by-passes that had been done a decade previously had, in fact, clogged. The skilled surgeon, whose name I can't remember, was able to create a new path around that blockage by placing a stent in another artery. Modern medical technology is a very impressive thing. My mother had died from a heart attack at the age of 49; my dad had passed away from a massive heart attack six months later, at the age of 53. I'm blessed to still be alive- much less racing!

Which, of course, is what I was doing, one month later- at Daytona? I think this is the race at which I only drove 15 minutes before turning the car over to Hector. It was a good strategy. We won.

A month after that it was time again to race at Moroso. But, for the first time, Hector had a conflict- and couldn't make the race. Not a problem, I assured everyone- I'd just do the hour and half race by myself.

Or, at least, I'd do the driving myself. Hector's dad, and my good friend from Pine Island, Dennis Sprague, agreed to help at the track, and to pit the car. They did their parts, and, I did my mine. I think I may have actually qualified on the pole. I know that I won. I was very, very proud of myself that night! Dennis and I celebrated at the only dining facility near our hotel- The KFC buffet! Highly recommended.

And, that's the way that the rest of the season went. Against admittedly limited competition, Hector and I won all of the remaining races. Our pit crew, Big Hector, Dennis, and Sherry were flawless throughout the entire season. As a team, we had our act together. A second consecutive Tropical Endurance Series Championship. And, the icing on the cake was that our results were so strong that we also won the SCCA's Southeastern Division Endurance Championship. Now, as silly racers are often wont to do, we decided that we needed a bigger challenge.

Actually, the new challenge was a very logical step to take. The SCCA had made a decision to transition to a third generation of the Spec Racer. The second generation car that we had been driving- powered by a 1.9 liter engine originally designed more than a decade earlier for the now out-of- production Ford Escort, was being replaced by a so-called "Gen 3" car. This new iteration of the Spec Racer continued to use the same chassis, suspension, brakes, and body. But, the new engine (and transmission) for the car was more powerful, and much lighter. The motor produced about 35 additional horsepower, and weighed roughly 150 pounds less. These may not sound like major changes, but when you realize that the engine being replaced only produced 105 horsepower, and the previous version of the car weighed only 1670 pounds, it's easy to see that these changes were transformative. For starters, the new car was much more fun to drive- the weight reduction allowed the car to become more responsive, and the additional power created a car that was now seriously quick. In addition to these two changes, the new car also came with a different required type of tire- one that was radial in design construction, and which featured a slick tread surface. These three changes created a car that was significantly faster, and quicker, than the previous generation car. It was, so to speak, a brand new ball game.

But, before we could begin to enjoy this new challenge we would have to rebuild our existing car to these new specifications. The SCCA had put together a conversion kit for this purpose- with a roughly $12,000 price tag. Sherry and I thought long and hard about whether we wanted to go down this path. After all we were retired, and money was tight. We easily could have just decided to sell everything, and to hang up the helmet. That, in fact, is probably what we should have done. But, at the end of the day we couldn't bring ourselves to do that. For my part, I didn't want to quit driving without having been able to race the new Gen 3 car. I relished being able to experience how it would handle- I guessed that it, in some ways, was going to resemble the light, responsive character of the original Spec Renault cars at, of course, a much higher rate of speed. I wanted to see what that felt like. I also reasoned that winning three consecutive TES championships would feel better than retiring having won just two!

Hector had volunteered, if I'd purchase the conversion kit, to provide the labor, and expertise, to build the new car. That saved at least $7,000 versus what we'd had have to pay for a prep shop to do the conversion. And, I knew that, not only would this be a cheaper alternative-I knew that if he did the work it would be done right.

A week later Hector and Anna's garage was filled with a Spec Racer that was being carefully torn down to the bare frame. We'd decided that if we were going to do the conversion that we should do a total rebuild. After all, the car had been originally built in 1985, over thirty years earlier. And, many of the parts on the car had never been changed. So, Hector stripped it down, and threw all the old stuff away. Then, with a few additional checks written, new parts began to arrive. He sent the chassis off to be sand blasted, and then powder coated. After much thought we eventually settled on a basic gloss black color for the frame. When it came back it looked spectacular- or, at least as spectacular as any conglomeration of welded square steel tubing can. We were glad that we'd done the right thing by our old reliable war horse.

Three long months later the work was finally done. Hector had labored in his garage spending long hours almost every evening assembling, and refitting, all the hundreds of pieces that made up the racecar. While this was going on we'd also had the body work repaired, and repainted. Now, it was all done, and it was time for the new season's first race- a one and a half hour enduro at Palm Beach. But, we didn't want to race the car without having first tested it. After all, everything on the car was new- we needed to make sure that it all worked, and that nothing would fall off. Fortunately, there was a test day scheduled at PBIR prior to that first race. We entered.

I seem to remember Hector and I discussing which of us should take the new car out for its first laps. I wanted Hector to do it since he'd done all the work on the car. He wanted me, the owner, to drive it. Truthfully, now, I don't really remember for sure which of us drove it first- but, I think he did. I do definitely remember, however, how the new car felt when I drove it.

For the first sessions in the morning we had decided to start the test on a set of left over tires from the previous season. We actually had to use these since the new style tires were still being mounted at the track. But, we also wanted to isolate the car's differences, without the confusion of a new type of tire thrown into the mix. And, honestly, I'm glad that we made that decision. My first session out was eye opening. The car was clearly faster, and quicker, in all respects. Immediately, without even pushing, or trying, I was several seconds faster than I'd ever gone in the old car. And, the reason for needing to upgrade the tires for the car was also obvious. The new engine's power immediately overwhelmed the old tires' ability to grip the track. As a result, the car was loose- very loose-when you powered out of the corners. If you didn't ease into the throttle the tail of the car of the car would instantly step out. Fun, but not fast. But, it was a great learning experience about just how different the revised car was.

For the afternoon session we bolted on a set of the new spec tires. Instantly, the edginess that we had experienced in the morning was gone. Now, we had levels of grip that we'd never had before- much higher levels of grip to go along with the increased power. It was now time to go fast! In fact, it quickly became obvious that the challenge now was to actually go fast enough to approach the limit of the new tires. It required unlearning hundreds of previous laps that we'd made around the track, and replacing that knowledge, and feel, with new sensations from laps that were about four seconds faster than we'd ever gone before. Our speeds down the straight were significantly faster, but the new tires allowed us to brake at roughly same distances as before. And, our speeds through the turns were all higher. Hector and I both left the track that night knowing that we'd not even yet begun to explore the limits of this new combination. But, we were both smiling- from ear to ear. The investment, and effort, had been worthwhile.

The next day's race was interesting. The new formula for our cars had brought some new competition out of the closet. Chief among the new competitors was Ron Inge, the nice guy out of Ft. Myers that I'd been racing against for as long as I'd been driving Spec Racers. Hector, too, had raced against Ron throughout his career. Ron always raced clean, and well. Some days he could be very quick- particularly at Moroso. And, this was one of those days. He qualified on the pole. We were second. And, that's the way we finished. For the first time in a very long while Caribbean Auto Racing had not won. I recall that some of our other competitors actually smiled about that. Truthfully, I could understand their reactions. It had been a long time since we'd been beaten.

The next race was at Daytona, a track that always drew a large field of cars. This year was no exception- I think that there were seven Gen 3 cars entered. One of these cars was being driven by none other than Hector's boss- John Tecce. His very quick co-driver was a customer of the company that Hector worked for- Jim Cox. Together they represented a serious challenge- not only for the overall win, but, more importantly, for "water cooler bragging rights" in Hector's shop.

As it turned out, an even quicker driver won the race. The Tecce/Cox car finished second, and we finished behind them- but, not without some controversy. Standing in the pits after I'd turned the car over to Hector, I timed the pit stop for our competitors to ensure that they satisfied the five minute minimum time requirement. This was routine- everyone timed each other's stops. In fact, it was not uncommon for teams to help each other with the timing when they had a watch, or operator, malfunction. But, in this case I was surprised when Tecce left the pits forty seconds too soon. I was sure that they were going to be penalized.

Days later, when the final results were released, I couldn't believe my eyes that the two lap penalty specified for a pit stop this short had not been applied. Tecce's car was still shown in second. Truthfully, I didn't care that much about the results- I knew that John and Jim weren't running for season points. But, what I did care about was understanding why the specified penalty hadn't been applied. Before every Enduro race the drivers are lectured, at length, by the Race Steward about the required minimum time for pit stops in which refueling takes place, and reminded about the severe penalties that would be levied should that required minimum time not be met. In the years that we'd been running Enduros our team had always been fastidious in ensuring that our stops met the required minimum time. I didn't care about protesting the results; I just wanted to understand how they'd gotten away with it so that we might be able to use the same trick at the next race. So, several days later I called the Steward, and asked what had happened.

He referred me to the Head of Timing and Scoring. At this point I should mention that the SCCA is an all volunteer organization. All Stewards, all Officials, all Workers, are volunteers. Nobody is being paid- they do what they do for fun, and for the love of the sport. Consequently, nobody expects to receive a lot of criticism. And, I totally understand, and respect, that. But, it did take a while for me to convince those to whom I spoke that I truly wasn't being critical- I simply wanted to understand what had happened, and why.

What I eventually learned from the pleasant lady who ran Timing and Scoring was very informative. I knew that determining whether the measured minimum time for a pit stop is met is calculated by adding five minutes to the required transit time for a car traveling at the maximum allowed pit lane speed to cover one half of the length of pit lane, and then adding that sum to the fastest measured lap time for that car over the course of the race. This sum is then compared with all the lap times for that car over the course of the race. If the stop met the required minimum time then one lap time during the race would have to meet, or be longer than, this calculated minimum required time. This procedure worked fine as long as the race was run under green flag conditions. But, if a car had come into the pits before a full course yellow had been displayed, and left the pits while the full course caution was still out, then it was possible that the calculation would not show the true length of the pit stop. That is what had happened with the Tecce/Cox car. They had entered the pits for the stop just before the yellow flag was displayed. The yellow was still out when their car had exited the pits. The subsequent yellow flag lap had been so slow that there was no way, using this technique, to determine whether the pit stop itself had actually been too quick.

I was unhappy, but could clearly understand what had happened. The only thing I could do was suggest that eventually they should measure, using the timing transponders with which all cars are equipped, the actual times taken to traverse the full length of the pits and to make the pit stop.

She replied that that methodology had actually been tested at the race in question, but that the new methodology had not been approved for use at that race. I complimented her on having pursued this new technology, and suggested, possibly somewhat grumpily, that it be put in place as soon as possible. I was delighted to see that the next time we came to that track this new technique was, in fact, in use. I like to think that my attention to this issue may have played a small part in bringing about this important change.

The increased level of competition meant that we were not going to dominate the season as we had done the previous year. We were still in the running for the championship, but the outcome was likely going down to the final race of the year. Working against us was the fact that, due to the requirements of his real job, Hector was only able to make a few of that year's races. Working for us was the fact that our strongest competitor, Ron Inge, might not run all of that year's races either. And, as it turned out, that's the way the championship ended. Since Ron missed two races, we easily took the championship- our third in a row.

I had been racing for almost thirty years. For much of that time my results had been, essentially, mid-pack. I felt that I had, for the most part, always been a good racer. I may not have ever been the fastest guy on the track (usually about two seconds per lap from glory), but I generally knew what I was doing, and why. But, every racer ultimately wants to win, and most want to be a champion. Running the Tropical Endurance Series allowed me to finally accomplish both of those things, and provided comfort, and closure, on the efforts of a lifetime.

I especially want to thank a couple of people who were critical to this accomplishment. Hector de la Torriente, was my co-driver, crew chief, mechanic, truck driver, and driving coach. Without his assistance none of this would have been possible. His wife, my step-daughter, Anna, also needs a great deal of thanks for the role she played in allowing Hector and

I to do what we did. We appropriated her garage for four years, and took Hector away from home for far, far, too many days. A special thanks also needs to go to Hector's dad, Hector de la Torriente, Sr. I don't think he missed a single race over this entire period. He was a vital member of our pit crew- either helping to fuel the car, or to time our stops. He made a big difference. Another critical part of our pit crew, especially, in the last two years, was the contribution made by Dennis Sprague, and his wife, Carolyn. These neighbors in St. James City became vital members of the team. For the last two years Dennis was the team's chief re-fueler-dressing out in a fireproof suit, gloves and helmet- ensuring that our re-fueling stops were always flawless. I need to mention that Dennis performed these duties at one race even as he was suffering in severe pain from what eventually turned out to be a near fatal intestinal rupture.

And, finally I have to thank, from the bottom of my heart, the assistance provided by my wife, Sherry. Her primary role at the track was to time our pit stops. As a result, we never screwed up a stop- never received a penalty for a short stop, and never spend any unnecessary time in the pits. But, her role did not end there. When necessary, she could put on the crew chief's radio headset, and play that role superbly, too. She knew what she was doing. One example of this was at the final race at Homestead. This race had been shortened by fifteen minutes from the normal ninety minutes. For some reason, I had failed to realize the potential opportunity this change in race length provided- we might not need to refuel to finish the race. We'd still have to make a five minute stop, but if we didn't add fuel, the driver wouldn't have to get out of, and get back into, the car. Neither would the team need to remove the bodywork from the car to access the fuel filler. Sherry noticed that one of our competitors had already elected to pursue this strategy, and relayed that information to me. She then asked if we wanted to do this also? I quickly realized that, given the five minutes that we'd be stationary in the pits, that we'd only need to actually run seventy minutes of track time-

and hour and ten minutes. While this was longer than we'd ever run in the new car without refueling, we'd seen one of our competitors run longer than that at an earlier race. Together we quickly made the decision to not refuel, taking away one of the primary opportunities for a mistake. It was a good call, and good work on her part to have spotted the opportunity.

Sherry has been with me for all of the years that we have spent at the track. There is no way that I can adequately thank her for all that she's done- both at the track, and away from it. But, I want her to know that I appreciate it, and that I love her very much.

Gen 2 Spec Racer Ford: Homestead Front Straight.

Author enters Homestead's Turn 1 at full speed in Gen 2 Spec Racer.

Gen 2 Spec Racer Ford: Homestead Turn 3. Author clips apex tightly!

Celebrating Gen 3 Spec Racer's first victory. Palm Beach Int. Raceway. Hector De La Torriente, Dennis Sprague, and Mitch Grant standing in front of car.

Author drives Daytona high banks in Gen 2.

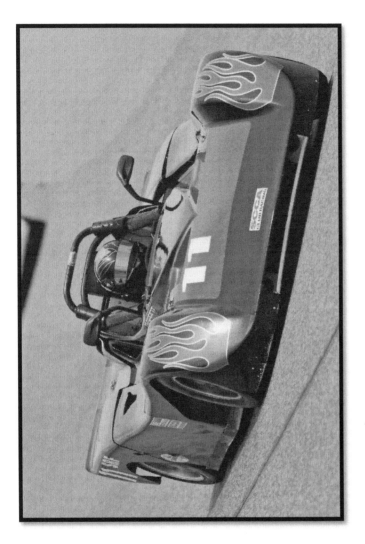

Author enters Homestead NASCAR 3 at full speed in Gen 2 Spec Racer Ford.

Gen 3 Spec Racer's first outing at Palm Beach International Raceway.

Author relaxes in Gen 2 prior to qualifying at Homestead.

Book Five: Dies Irae- LIber Scriptus.

"The written book shall be brought

In which all is contained

Whereby the world shall be judged..."

Chapter Twenty Nine: The Tracks At Which We Ran

Any record such as this should, it seems, include a record of all the different tracks at which I was blessed to race (either as a driver, crew chief, or both). They are listed, as well as my memory will allow, in the order in which I first ran them. In addition to a mere listing of the tracks, I've also tried to include a summary of my thoughts about the track, and in some cases, a description of what it was like to drive some of the tracks' most memorable corners.

Sebring, Florida- Skip Barber Short Course

This was the location at which I took my Skip Barber training. The track was really nothing more than portions of the front and back straights of the twelve hour track, linked at one end by cone-marked cross over roads, and at the other by a portion of Sebring's infamous Turn Seventeen. The back side of the course featured a number of slow speed turns, created by cones, and designed to feature important teaching points for the school. Two things I remember about the track.

First, some of the course was laid out across the old runways of the air base. Standing and simply looking at these sections you would swear that the turns were perfectly flat. But, if you looked closer, and changed perspective by getting down on your hands and knees, you could actually see that the track was significantly cambered- the original runway had been built in this fashion to facilitate drainage in its former use as an air base. This camber was probably close to two feet in either direction. The School actually used this feature to instruct about the concept of vertical corners (also, I should proudly note, mentioned in Taruffi's book). Turning the car into this camber was like driving onto a banked corner. The upward slope provided by the camber generated additional traction as the tires were forced into the surface. This allowed you to corner faster. But, driving off of this cambered surface produced the opposite effect. When the track fell away from the car, grip was significantly reduced. I vividly remember learning about this effect as I spun, at a very high rate of speed, exiting this corner. It was a good lesson- drivers always need to pay attention to the camber of the road's surface.

The second thing that I recall about that little track was the challenge of the course's first turn. It was about a seventy-five degree bend at the end of the front straight. With guts and practice, it could be taken at full speed. It took me a while, but eventually, I was able to do it flat. This turn came to be my favorite corner. I learned then I liked fast corners- as long as there wasn't much to hit on the exit.

Sebring, Florida- Twelve Hour, (and Club) Course:

As referenced earlier- this track was where I made my official racing debut. Over the years, I have probably raced at this track, with its many different configurations, more than any other. I like to joke that I have more laps around this place than anyone. Certainly, I've raced there a lot.

To this day, its character remains the same as when it was first used in the early 1950's. It's dirty, bumpy, flat, fast, fun, usually hot, and, surprisingly, challenging. It remains a direct throw back to the earliest days of sports car racing in the United States. You can race today on the same surfaces, and in some cases, drive the same corners, raced on by such track gods as Juan Fangio, Phil Hill, and hundreds of others. I'm convinced that the facility may actually be haunted by the spirits of these heroes. If, on a quiet evening as the sun begins to set, you walk up the pit straight and into the first corner, and then listen carefully, you may hear, as I have, their voices...... You can make up your own mind about this, but.... I've actually had conversations there with drivers from the past. I can tell you that they have very high expectations, and little regard for "racing's posers." My sense was that the pit straight was quite crowded with the spirits of those types of pretenders. The real racers' ghosts were found out on the track- especially in Turn One.

Turn One at Sebring 12 Hour is one of road racing's great corners. It is a fast left hander with a total change in direction in excess of one hundred degrees. But, despite the acuteness of the corner, the width of the track going into the corner allows drivers to enter the corner at a higher rate of speed than one would otherwise assume. In our Spec Racers we were able to enter the corner at a speed in excess of ninety miles per hour. Adding to the corner's difficulty, at turn-in, is the fact that the actual apex of the turn is visually hidden behind guardrails and fencing on the inside of the corner. And, if that doesn't create enough of a challenge, the track's width narrows dramatically, into just a two lane road, as you exit the corner. In other words, your room for error, as you now travel in excess of one hundred miles per hour, has been greatly reduced. Evidence of just how tricky this can be is shown by the dirt that lines the outside side of the track at exit, churned bare by the tires of unlucky racers who have slid wide. And, slightly further down the track, by dozens of lurid black skid marks that cross the track, right to left. Some of these rubber trails can be seen to culminate in ugly black smudges on the left-side guard rails- clear evidence about the real danger of TTO (Trailing Throttle Oversteer) that Skip Barber's staff always warned against. But, all of these challenges are what makes this a great corner- if you do it well. Taking it successfully requires going to full power only shortly after the car has turned into the corner- well before you can to see either the corner's apex, or its track out point. To do this requires what is known in the trade as "commitment!" Good drivers really stand out here. One of my most vivid memories of observing this kind of commitment in this corner was standing on the outside of the turn and watching as a then young, fearless Dorsey Schroeder hammered, and drifted a Roush Mustang thorough this turn.

Another noteworthy corner at Sebring is the track's famous "Hairpin" turn. During the circuit's first three decades the "Hairpin" was the classic definition for this type of corner. It was located at the end of a long, high-speed straightaway. The turn itself was an acute corner to the right- it probably changed direction by at least one hundred and thirty degrees! The curving straight that led to the corner allowed cars to nearly reach their top speeds, but the "Hairpin" could only be taken at a much slower speed- approximately 30 miles per hour. This layout created one of the very best braking areas in the world. Eventually, the lack of adequate runoff room beyond the turn, for any cars that might suffer sudden brake failure, necessitated the redesign of this corner into what is now, somewhat condescendingly, known as the "Safety Pin." The turn was moved a couple of hundred feet further up the track, and the layout itself was modified slightly. But, still the corner remains one of the racing world's greatest braking zones. There is something about the thrill of approaching this turn in fifth gear, not applying the brakes until somewhere around the 350 yard mark. Then, in the next several hundred yards, or so, scrubbing off about one hundred miles per hour, while downshifting from fifth, to fourth, to third, to second gears- usually while trying to pass at least one car that you are racing against, before turning in, while trail-braking, deeply into the corner. Then, as you approach the apex, you begin to aggressively squeeze the gas pedal towards the floor, setting up an all-out sprint to the next corner. I have so many great memories of that corner!

The track's other signature corner is the legendary "Turn Seventeen," the final corner on the track. Conceptually, the turn seems simple enough- it links two sections of old runway with opposite directions of travel, i.e., in total, a one hundred and eighty degree corner. You might expect, given this extreme required change of direction that the speed through the corner would be slow. But, that is not the case. In reality, the corner is neither simple, nor slow. In fact, entry into the turn is usually taken at full speed. Drivers then brake aggressively, and shift down two gears, before rotating at over eighty miles per hour into the turn's midpoint. And, then, once the car is settled, drivers go back to full throttle, exiting the corner well in excess of a hundred miles per hour.

As mentioned above, and depending upon the type of car that your are driving, you enter the corner, which follows a nearly mile long straight and is nothing more than a slight bend to the right, at full-speed- in our car, close to one hundred and forty miles per hour. Then as you approach the tip of the inside concrete wall you begin to brake hard, shifting from fifth, to fourth, and finally, to third gear. As soon as you are into third, the car will hopefully have already rotated slightly to the right, helping you to make the next part of the corner. Then, you go back to full throttle. Of course, you can't actually slam the throttle wide open, but neither do you want to lose too much time easing it back to wide open- The difference being a fraction of a second-at the most. From that point on, assuming you have lined up properly for the apex and track-out points, you don't want to again lift the throttle. You want to hold it wide open. As Mick Robinson explained to me one day, when discussing this corner: "Just don't worry about it. You'll give up before the car will!"

There's only one other aspect to this corner that requires discussion- and that is its bumps! There are several massive bumps in the middle of this corner- bumps that, if not allowed for, can actually cause the car to leave the ground. And, obviously, trying to corner a car at nearly a hundred miles per hour with no tires actually touching the road is never a good thing. My only advice to avoiding the worst of the bumps is to avoid getting either too close to the inside of the track, or too wide in the turn, as you go under the bridge. My aiming point has always been about 1/3 of the way out from the inside of the bridge. But, if you are trying to pass another car in the middle of the turn, you can't always be so careful. Yahoo! Sebring is a classic track in all respects.

Palm Beach County Fairgrounds

This was a temporary circuit laid out around a fair grounds. It was about 1.6 miles in length. It was used only for a short period, I believe, from 1988 to 1990. It was primarily constructed to host CART, and IMSA races. We ran it in Firestone Firehawk as a preliminary to the IMSA race in 1990. The track was made up of sections of parking lot, and surface streets. I remember it being very much of a "squirt and shoot" type of circuit, with only one section, towards the end of the lap, being fast. Given that its design rewarded "technical" driving, I actually enjoyed it. But, once was enough. This is where Mike Scharnow totaled the Shelby Dodge that we were racing that year. I don't feel the need to say anything more about this track.

Miami Grand Prix- Bi-Centennial Park

I loved this circuit! For starters, its two mile layout along the Miami waterfront was beautiful- palm trees, cruise ships, yachts, sparkling turquoise water, gentle breezes, Latin music and food, and lots and lots of spectators. But, beyond that the track's layout just seemed to suit me.

Because it was a temporary street circuit, it was tightly lined with concrete barriers- in other words there was little room for error. It seemed to me that a careful driver was not at as much of a disadvantage at this track as he was at some other courses. It seems to me that a portion of the layout wound around, and alongside, a wharf, with each leg of the track a couple of hundred yards in length. These sections were connected

237

with tight turns at either end. This layout rewarded technical driving, and trail braking- both skills that I like to think I possessed. I vividly remember having a great deal of fun negotiating my way around this particular portion of the track. But, the back side of the track featured a very high speed sweeper that led onto a long stretch of Biscayne Boulevard. Once I learned that I could do this sweeper flat, I loved this section as well. It was a great track for me. I wish we could have run there more than once.

Topeka, Kansas- Heartland Park

At the time we raced at this track it was only about a few years old. None of us knew much about it, but we'd heard good things. Its front straight incorporated a portion of a drag strip, and then it wound around a series of hills, and valleys, before emptying onto the back straight. That fast stretch was broken up by an irritatingly tight chicane, which was then followed quickly by a section that linked back to the front straight. It didn't take many laps on the track for me to conclude that the attractiveness of the circuit had been oversold- it had too many chicanes, and not enough fast, challenging corners, for my taste. I'm glad that we only had to race there once.

Road Atlanta

This track, on the other hand, would make any driver regret that they'd ever complained about a track not having enough fast, challenging corners. In its original configuration, this place would quickly separate the men from the boys! I'll never forget the first lap that I made at this track in one of our Hondas. As I climbed from the car I was literally shaking. The speed of the track, and its layout, was unlike anything that I'd ever experienced before. For starters, the track was located in the foothills of the North Georgia Mountains. For a Florida boy, used to racing only on flat land, the added element of having to drive up, down, and over a mountain while racing was a significantly intimidating factor. The fact that there sometimes seemed to be nothing beyond the guardrail other than a deep drop into a valley took this flatlander a while to ignore.

The other element that I found intimidating at this track was its high speed nature – this was a very fast place, with few of the slow technical corners that I had previously been attracted to. When I finished my first session in the car, I knew that I needed help. Fortunately, one of our ex-drivers, Cass Whitehead, was an instructor at this track. I immediately went in search for him, as soon as I was out of the car. When I found him, I said: "Cass, I need help. I don't know what I'm doing here. How do I get around this damn place?"

He quickly realized, either from what I had said, the way that I'd said it, or from the color of my complexion, that I did, indeed, need an intervention. He suggested that we retire to the quietness of the team's trailer for debriefing and instruction.

There were three corners that required significant attention. The first was Turn One- a high speed bend to the right, at the end of the front straight. This corner transitioned into a steeply uphill section that was quickly followed by a slower, almost chicane-like, left/right/left section of track. Cass carefully talked me into understanding that the first corner only required a very short period of braking, just enough to facilitate a downshift. Then, as soon as the car was settled the driver turned into the corner, aiming for an apex at the very inside of the track that was just beyond the pedestrian bridge that spanned the track. Then, surprisingly, Cass told me to floor the accelerator and not move the steering wheel again until the car had crested the following hill, and neared the braking point for the following section. He stressed, that If I did that, I would be perfectly positioned for the following section. He was right.

The next section where intervention was required was the section of track at the end of the mile long back stretch known as "The Dip!" Cars at the end of a mile long straight away are, of course, going very, very fast. The Dip was a section of track that crested a slight rise, then sloped steeply downwards and bent to the left. This was followed by a bend back to the right, and a hill that sloped steeply upwards- all of the above, still taken at full speed. INTIMIDATING! Cass convinced me that all I had to do to drive this section was to turn in at full speed, hold my line, and then repeat this for the next section to the right. He advised that I not worry about any overtaking traffic. He advised that I should just let them deal with getting around as best they could.

There was no question that this was a frightening section of track, but, it was not nearly as intimidating as what came next.

Coming out of The Dip you charged up a steep hill, at full speed, pedal still flat to the floor, unable to see anything other than clear sky beyond the crest. Do you remember the term "Commitment?!" A vehicle bridge crossed over the track at the crest of the hill. Fortunately, some of the lettering on this bridge provided a convenient aiming point for drivers. The track itself began to arc to the right, just beyond the crest of the hill- but, drivers could not see any of this, given how steeply the track fell away on the back side of the hill. All of this meant that a driver needed to aim his car as it went under the bridge just slightly away from the inside of the track. If you did this correctly, when you popped over the top of the hill, at nearly full-speed, you would be on the left edge of the track, properly positioned for dealing with the following Turn Twelve- one of the most frightening corners in all of racing.

Beyond the hill, the track bent to the right, and sloped steeply downhill. This then led to an extremely fast, right handed corner at the very bottom of the hill. This corner then fed onto the front straight. Therefore, it was critical to carry as much speed thorough it as possible. And, the fact that it was squarely in front of everyone in the pits only added to the corner's challenge.

This layout by itself would be difficult enough, but to add to the difficulty, the outside of this corner, only a few yards off the track, was lined with a tall, imposing, solid concrete wall- a vertical embankment that supported the pit area which overlooked the track. The only protection provided for errant cars impacting this looming wall were just a few tire bundles.

In other words, this corner presented the driver with the ultimate racing dilemma- the need to go as fast as possible around the corner (ideally, in fact, to go flat out), but faced with the consequence of almost certainly impacting an unyielding concrete barrier should you screw up the turn. **Commitment!** Do you remember that term?

Road Atlanta has been modified over the years- the biggest change being replacing "The Dip" with a slower, less threatening, chicane. But, the course's fundamental nature, and challenge, remain. It is a wonderful track.

Mid Ohio

Set in the beautiful rolling farmland of central Ohio, this track is one of America's greatest racing venues. It has a little bit of everything- technical corners, fast sweeps, long straights, great spots for overtaking, elevation changes, beautiful scenery, and great viewing areas filled with passionate knowledgeable fans. It is a very enjoyable place to race. The only thing that keeps it from being a truly great place to race is its lack of at least one dangerous, fast, challenging, defining corner.

In my opinion one of the track's best corners is Turn One- a fast, ninety degree sweeper to the left at the end of the front straight. In our cars we were close to ninety miles per hour through this corner, at the very top end of third gear. Lightly brake before the turn, drop a gear, and then turn in, aiming for an apex point towards the end of the curbing on the inside that separates the track from cars exiting pit lane. As soon as you've turned in, then it's power down hard until you get to the end of the next straightaway. I've always thought that this was one of the most enjoyable corners in racing.

Another of my favorite turns here was the "Ski Jump Turn." This section of the track comes at the end of all the tight squiggly stuff on the back side of the course. The "Ski Jump" comes at the exit of this right-handed bend. The track slopes upward at this point, and the resulting brow prevents you from actually being able to see the edge of the track where you need to track out. This lack of vision requires the driver to aim at a point that he believes will allow him to fly over the crest of the hill upon exit and still land safely at the desired track out point on the edge of the track. Again, commitment- and fun!

Watkins Glen

This track represents the spiritual birthplace of road racing in America. Following WWII, the first SCCA road races in the US were held on the streets of the village of Watkins Glen. This beautiful little town sits, at the foot of the Finger Lakes Region, alongside the southern end of gorgeous Lake Seneca. The first race in the town, on a 6.6 mile long course laid out on public roads (most of which are still drivable today), was held in 1948. It was a great place to race back then, and it remains a great place to race today!

After a series of tragic accidents during races through the village, a decision was made to build a purpose built racetrack on the top of a tall hill outside of town. That track, built in 1956, remains as a portion of the track that is raced on today. In my mind, this circuit is one of America's greatest race tracks.

This "new" track, of course, also has tremendous history. It was the home of the United State Grand Prix for twenty years. Beyond that, the track has hosted just about every type of road racing series that has ever taken place in the U.S.- Can Am, Trans Am, FIA Sports cars, Indy Cars, NASCAR, SCCA Club racing, and, of course, Firestone Firehawk Endurance Racing.

When we were doing this series this track actually hosted the Series' only twenty four hour enduro. Caribbean Motorsports did two of these races. These events represent for me some of the highlights of my entire racing career- not because of our results. But, rather, because of the difficulty, money, and effort that were required. That, and the fact that we managed to have one of our cars finish each of the races we entered. Yeah!

The track sits on top of a mountain, surrounded by beautiful New York farms, picturesque rural scenes, and a gorgeous distant view of Lake Seneca. Because of its mountain top location the track is subject to extremes in weather. I like to joke, based on my experiences at the track, that it always rains at Watkins Glen.

For this portion of the book, I should again mention that the two times that I've been most scared in a race car took place at this track. The first of these, as I've already discussed, spinning out and being stopped at midnight absolutely in the middle of track at the high speed Turn Five during my first twenty four hour race. Fortunately, no damage was done, and we were able to continue- but, I definitely saw, for the first time, my life pass before my eyes.

The other uber-scary moment at that track occurred when I was driving for the first time in the rain, in one of the team's CRXs. Even at the best of times, rearward visibility from these cars was marginal. But, if you add in rain, the windows and mirrors misting over, it was simply impossible to see out the back of those cars. That condition does not make for an enjoyable outing in a relatively slow race car. When I got out of the car after the session, Bill Wilkins told me that I was as white as a ghost!

The one section of track that I want to mention further is the section known as "The Uphill Esses." This left/right/left/right section of track follows Turn Two, and is fast, uphill, narrow, and tightly bounded on both sides by unforgiving steel, and concrete, guardrails. Even in our CRXs we were doing one hundred miles per hour through this turn. This is no place to get careless, especially in traffic. In the twenty four hour race all three Firehawk classes, with vastly different top speeds, ran together in the race- Grand Sports (150 mph); Sports (140 mph); and Touring (130 mph). So it was not uncommon to be going through the esses surrounded by faster cars anxious to get past. Fortunately, though, we never had any issues there.

Road America

This track, without question, is the greatest of America's road racing tracks. Its history dates back to the 1950's when, like at Watkins Glen, sports car races were run through the streets of the village of Elkhart Lake, Wisconsin. At that time, this beautiful little town was a renowned summer vacation destination for the wealthy citizens of Milwaukee and Chicago, who tried to escape the heat of those cities by ascending to the delightful resorts that fringed the village's clear, cool lake.

After the tragedy at Watkins Glen in 1952, where a child was killed by an errant racing machine, laws were changed to ban races on public highways. As a result, a local citizen, Cliff Tufte, organized a group of local citizens who developed a plan to build a permanent racecourse on 525 acres of Wisconsin farmland outside the town of Elkhart Lake. The track utilized the natural topography of the area's glacial Kettle Moraine region, sweeping around rolling hills and plunging through natural ravines. At 4 miles in length, with 14 turns, the track today is virtually the same as when it was first constructed. It is still revered around the world as one of racing's finest, and most challenging, road courses. It was first used for racing on September 10-11, 1955. That event was won by Phil Hill in a Ferrari Monza, who beat Sherwood Johnson, in a D- type Jaguar, by an eyelash.

For me, what makes this track so special is that it features some of everything that makes road racing great, all laid out in a scenic natural environment. It features three different straights- each of which is long enough for a car to reach its terminal velocity- followed by great braking zones. It also features a number of tight technical corners, most of which are laid out to incorporate elevation and camber changes. And, critically, it has what is possibly the fastest, most dangerous, and most intimidating, corner in all of American racing- known simply as "The Kink."

This turn, which comes approximately one third of the way down the longest and fastest straight on the track, is a simple, forty five degree bend to the right. At the point where cars encounter this corner they are approaching their top speed- speed that for a good lap time needs to be carried down the remainder of the long straight that follows. A corner like this, flat and fast, would normally be intimidating enough. But, this turn is closely bordered, on both sides, by unyielding concrete and Armco- guard rails that are scarred from frequent high speed encounters with out of control race cars. Taking this corner too fast will almost always result in a serious crash- against either the outside, or the inside barrier, or both.

Such a crash will, without question, seriously damage the car. It also has the potential to seriously damage the driver of said vehicle. I've never met anyone who didn't have serious respect for this section of track. "The Kink" represents the ultimate dilemma for a driver- the necessity to carry maximum speed down the following straight, set against the likelihood of incurring serious injury and/or damage should the turn's limits be exceeded.

For me, this corner represented the ultimate racing challenge. I can still remember that every time I came out of the preceding turn onto the straight that led to The Kink, my eyes would automatically focus far ahead where the road disappeared to the right, and then, involuntarily, my chest would tighten. I had heard other drivers brag that they could take this corner without lifting, and I knew that if I could do this that there were seconds of lap time to be gained. I badly wanted to be able to take this corner flat. But, despite the instructions to not lift that my brain gave every time I approached this corner- my right foot, for some reason, never actually got that message. I was normally very, very close to taking the corner flat, breathing the throttle only the slightest amount, but I would be not being truthful if I claimed that I had ever taken this corner without lifting. Decisions like these, of course, are what led to my lap times usually being two seconds off the pole sitter's. But, I was also always able to bring the car home in one piece.

Laguna Seca

Another classic American track, built in the mid-1950's after racing was also banned on the roads of nearby Pebble Beach. The track is built to run around, and over, a steep, rocky, windswept hill. As a result the track features an elevation change, from highest point to lowest, of 180 feet. Originally, the track was situated on the US Army's Fort Ord. In 1974 the track was deeded to Monterey County Parks Department. It continues to be part of the park system, which leads to very stringent noise limits being placed on the track. The track is currently 2.2 miles long. Its signature corner is the world famous downhill-plunging "Corkscrew" Turn 8.

Caribbean Motorsports raced at this track twice- 1992 and 1993, but I never actually drove this track. Mike and Mark Scharnow ran together in 1992, and in 1993 we ran Lance and Mitch in one car, and Dan Nye and Luis Sanchez in the other. In 1993, our lead car developed electrical issues. As a consequence, Lance was inserted in the second car. As the race unfolded we actually thought that he had managed to unlap himself, and had even possibly won the race. But, a late full course caution caused by our lead car stopping on track once again due to electrical issues (talk to Sherry) caused a great deal of confusion, and eventually relegated us to 4th place. As it turned out this was actually fortunate- impound inspected the transmissions on the first three cars, which were all found to be legal. Ours, on the other hand, might not have passed this review.

Portland International Raceway

This 2 mile long track, on the outskirts of Portland, Oregon, features 12 turns. The track is perfectly flat, and runs clockwise. The front straight uses the facility's drag strip, and features a tight chicane at the end. From there the track, which is laid out roughly like a triangle, winds towards the back of the park, before heading towards the front with another long fast straight, followed by a very quick series of left-right turns that then dump back onto the front straight.

I drove the track in 1992 in the CMS Honda Civic Si. I remember spinning twice coming on to the front straight (well, at least I was trying, right?). I also recall being extremely overheated when I got out of the car.

In 1993, Lance and Mitch won the race in our Honda Prelude. This was probably the most difficult race that we ever won, since I'd managed to miscommunicate with Mitch about when to pit. As a result, Lance had to start at the back of the field. But, despite this disadvantage, he was not to be denied- he passed the whole field to win. A huge performance by "The Race God." Our second car finished a strong third.

Savannah- Roebling Road Raceway

A 2.0 mile facility with 9 turns located on the outskirts of Savannah, Georgia. We tested our Hondas there one weekend. I also did a SCCA driving school at the track as I transitioned into SCCA racing. I believe I also did one SCCA regional race at the track. No real highlights to report.

Daytona International Speedway

I have been blessed to have spent much of my life around this amazing facility, both as a spectator, and as a driver. This so-called "World's Center of Racing" was built in 1959, primarily as an oval track upon which NASCAR's stock cars could run. But, it also incorporated an infield track which, when combined with portions of the oval, measures 3.56 miles in length. It was on this track that I drove many races in the Spec Ford. The highlights for me had to be starting on the Pole Position three separate times (Hector qualified the car, not me), and winning, with Hector's help, several times at this track.

My first experience at the track had been attending the 1965 Daytona Continental with my father. That was a huge year in the track's history given the beginning of Ford's assault on endurance racing in the form of the Ford GT, and Shelby Cobra, programs. I still have vivid memories of standing on the inside of Turn 1, and watching as pole sitter Lloyd Ruby, driving the Ford GT, managed to overshoot the first corner, of the first lap. He recovered, however, and with Ken Miles, went on to win that race. I also remember the awesome display that the Shelby Daytona Cobras put on in this race. The two cars ran just feet apart for the majority of the race. I also recall watching from the pits as Walt Hansgen's Ferrari 365 P2 exploded its engine as it tried to slow for Turn 1. That caused a mess. I very much enjoyed watching that race- as I did the dozens of other 24 hour races thereafter that at which I was a spectator.

Driving this track was one of the great highlights of my racing career. Coming out of NASCAR Turn 4 at full speed, and seeing ahead what looked like a mile of additional straight away was always a highlight. Our Gen 3 cars would reach nearly 150 miles per hour on this portion of the track. This straight eventually led to the banked Tri-Oval corner located in the middle of the grandstands. Generally, in our car we would enter this section low on the track, and then drift upwards towards the outside wall. The objective of this was to be able to begin our turn in to the corner from near the outer edge of the track. This approach defined the so called "Fast Car Line." Another approach was simply to stay along the inside of the track before turning in. For me the "Fast Car Line" seemed to create a smoother faster entry, and allowed you to go deeper into the turn before braking. The difficulty of this corner, regardless of which line was used, was the lack of good marker points to define the turn-in, and braking points. Turn-in was not so bad- you basically just turned as soon as the corner lined up for you. For me, the proper braking point was more difficult to identify. I generally went to the brakes as soon as I crossed a lighter colored section of pavement that indicated that I was coming off of the banking and onto the infield. It was always important to not brake too late for this corner- and, this, given no clear, precise braking point, was easy to do. I found that the best way for me to do the corner was to brake and downshift late enough that I needed to consciously trail brake into the apex of the turn. Keeping weight on the nose of the car here was always important since the road is actually severely crowned. You need to make sure, as you are braking and setting up for the turn to the apex, that you stay on the left side of that crown- otherwise, you will always slide wide of the apex. The apex point itself is actually a little past, and very tight, to the leading edge of the inside guard rail. You need to be able to make that apex so that you can go back to full throttle as quickly as possible. If you're wide, you won't be able to do that. Generally, you will always find yourself embedded with multiple other cars going through this corner. There is no one right way to get through it in traffic, but in general the first car able to go to, and hold, full power will prevail. But, you have to be careful here- there are always a lot of accidents in this section- frequently, because of cars braking too deeply for the corner. But, also because of too many cars trying to go through the one lane exit at the same time. Care and anticipation are required in this section.

Another fun part of the track is the "Kink," a full speed sweeper on the infield portion of the track. The turn-in is at an almost invisible spot where the track's inner edge begins to go straight at the same time that the main track turns to the corner. Hard to explain- but easy. Care needs to be taken here to not let the car drift too far to the right as you exit the turn- you are going to need to quickly work back to the left side to begin braking for the upcoming hairpin turn to the right. In our cars, the braking point was roughly one half of the way through the side road that intersects from the left side of the track. There are a couple of ways to line up for the entry into the hairpin. The difference being how far do you drift to the outside of the track before turning in? Either approach will work just fine as long as you don't early apex the hairpin. Use a late apex, and a lot of the inside curbing. The goal here is to compromise the corner so that you can accelerate as strongly as possible onto the straight leading to the next turn. This is critical since the following Turn Six can be a useful passing area. But, do not- I repeat, do not- become so focused on trying to pass someone here that you screw up your acceleration onto the banking of NASCAR's Turn One- you need to carry as much speed as possible onto the long, long straight.

The most challenging of the track's corners comes roughly two thirds of the way down the back stretch- "The Bus Stop Chicane." Carrying speed through this left/right/right/left section is critical to speed on the banking and homestretch, and is key to a good lap. In our cars we would brake hard at the 150 yard marker, before shifting down from fifth to fourth to third. I learned that I could use the curbing on all sections of this corner aggressively. As soon as you make the first turn in, and aim for the second, you can begin to feed in more, and more, power. You want to be at full power mid-corner, and then never, hopefully, lift as you turn in to the right/left parts of the chicane's exit. Use the curbing, and let the big boy eat!

The last thing to mention about Daytona is drafting which, even on the road course, is critical. A good draft will easily make up two, or maybe three, whole seconds of lap time. Drafting successfully is not an easy thing to do. Actually, the drafting itself is easy- but, being able to run close to another car, lap after lap, at full speed is not easy. But, this is what is necessary to being able to get into, and maintain, a good draft. You'll easily be able to feel the pull of the draft as you begin to close in on the rear of a similar speed vehicle. You can feel the suction, and care has to be taken to not let it pull you into the other car too aggressively. What you want to do then is just stick the nose of your car up under the back of the car in front, using the brake pedal if necessary to maintain the proper position, while the accelerator is nailed to the floor. But, when you approach the next braking area, i.e., Turn One, the following car will need to back away first. Otherwise, when the leading car applies its brakes the following car will plow into it. The following car needs to separate itself by a few feet, and then be prepared to brake at the same time as the leading car. Watching two or more drafting partners work together at Daytona is a sight to see. My driving partner, Hector de la Torriente, is a master at being able to do this- hence, his "The Daytona Dominator" nickname. He is as fast around Daytona as anyone.

If you ever get a chance to race at Daytona, do it!

Homestead- Miami Speedway

This track is built just to the east of Homestead, Florida. The track opened in 1995. It was constructed by Ralph Sanchez, the local who had previously promoted the extremely successful Miami Grand Prix races that ran through downtown Miami. It was conceived as part of a plan to help the Homestead area recover following the devastation to the area by Hurricane Andrew. The track reflects the art deco district of nearby Miami Beach with its liberal use of aqua, teal, purple and silver colors. Initially, the oval portion of the track was a smaller scale copy of the flat, four-turned Indianapolis Motor Speedway. But, it soon became apparent that its flat corners, and four ninety-degree turn geometry, made passing and racing difficult. In 1996, 1997, and again in 2003 the track was reconfigured away from the rectangular structure into a more traditional, continuous-turn oval- albeit with progressive banking in the turns. These modifications have turned it into one of NASCAR's favorite tracks.

The oval itself is 1.5 miles in length. The road course (there are actually two variations of the road course) measures 2.1, and 2.3, miles in length. Both of these configurations are wonderful to race on. The longer "Modified Road Course" incorporates all of NASCAR Turns Three and Four, and is the faster of the two. The shorter "Road Course" features a turn off of the back stretch onto a quick, and challenging, section of infield.

The most challenging, and fun, of the corners of either track configuration is Turn One. See Chapter One! I loved racing at Homestead. In addition to the previously mentioned Turn One, it featured several technical sections, and a hairpin with a great braking zone.

And, besides, the town itself features some great Cuban Food!!!!!!! We very much liked racing there.

Palm Beach International Raceway (formerly Moroso Motorsports Park)

This 2 mile road course is located east of Jupiter, Florida. It was originally built in 1964, and was intended at the time to become the home for the 12 Hour race traditionally held at Sebring. But, the track's location in a poorly drained, nearly swamp- like, area soon ruled out this aspiration. In 2008, the track was purchased by a new ownership group who completely remodeled it into a state of the art motorsports facility. The road course length is 2 miles, and features 12 turns.

We raced at this facility many times. Its essential character is that of a two long straights connected at either end by 180 degree roundabouts. There are a few other roundabouts thrown in for fun. The track is tough on your neck (sustained G forces), and tough on tires. The pavement's aggregate features a great deal of shell, which scrapes away at the tread of tires.

The Florida Region SCCA ran a large percentage of its races at this track since it was much less expensive to rent than the Homestead-Miami Speedway.

One of my fondest memories of this track is comparing my driving there to Hector's. Hector was, of course, usually quicker than me-frequently by two seconds. One of the great things about sharing a car with a co-driver is that it is relatively easy to compare driving. To facilitate that we were running a slick "Go-Pro" camera system mounted on the roll bar. After a race it was always fun to review the video of the race, and compare how each of us drove. In a nutshell, my driving was usually calm, precise, neat, smooth, technically correct, and unexciting. Hector's, on the other hand was forceful, impatient, aggressive, teetering on the edge, and always noticeably quicker. His video, when compared with mine, often seemed simply to be moving at a faster pace. As I studied where he made up his time it eventually dawned on me that he was always faster through the middle of the corners- he was continually pushing, carrying more speed, all the way through the corner. This is where he was closer to the limit; it was easy to see how his car would sometimes slide or step out, as he intentionally constantly challenged the bounds of control. My drives, on the other hand, were much smoother- I wasn't pushing the limits-especially through the middle of the corners.

Once this dawned on me I began to attempt to try to copy a little of Hector's technique. Gradually, this began to pay dividends, as evidenced by the fact that my lap times at Palm Beach began to get closer to his. I was very proud when, in one of our last races there that I was able to get to within less than a second of his best.

Barber Motorsports Park- Birmingham, Alabama

When Sherry and I moved from Atlanta to Birmingham, one of the things that we missed the most was our close access to the Road Atlanta race track. In 2000, the year of the move, there was no road racing anywhere in Alabama. But, this all changed in 2003 when this track opened. It was built by a wealthy dairyman, and real estate developer, by the name of George Barber. Mr. Barber was a onetime sports car racer, and avid motorcycle collector. He actually now owns the largest collection of racing motorcycles in the world. Eventually, this collection had outgrown the downtown-Birmingham warehouses where it was stored. He therefore decided to build an amazing facility on the outskirts of town, not only to house his collection, but also to provide a track on which to exercise the machines. And, while he was at it he decided to go ahead and ensure that the track would be able to accommodate automobile racing- at the highest level.

The track is a 15 turn, 2.4 mile complex. It was designed by renowned circuit architect Alan Wilson. The track was built to meet the highest level specifications for tracks in the world- i.e., F1 standards. The compact layout runs in a clockwise direction, and features a great number of elevation changes. The track is unusual in that there is no general access spectator seating at the start-finish line. Instead, the track relies on a large number of natural hill sides that overlook the track's key corners. Barber wanted the track to set new standards for motorsports facilities. Towards that end he was obsessive about the quality of the track's surface. He actually insisted that the track be repaved several times before it eventually met his standard for perfection. In addition, he wanted the grounds of the facility to be immaculate and beautiful. His goal was that his track should be regarded as the "Augusta National of Race Courses." Towards that end, he had planted a wide variety of azalea's and other types of flowering shrubs around the track. And, interspersed throughout the grounds were a large number of Mr. Barber's own artistic bronze sculptures. It's an impressive, world class, facility. And, that's just the race track itself.

The real highlight is the Barber Vintage Motorsport Museum. The museum has almost 1,500 vintage and modern motorcycles and racing cars. It is considered to be the largest motorcycle museum in the world. It also houses the world's largest collection of Lotus race cars.

The museum has been expanded since we were there last. Now, it is approximately twice as large as when it was first built. It even features a bridge that extends from the museum out over the track itself.

I always enjoyed driving this track. While the track was relatively tight and technical, it was, given the track's design and layout, still a challenge to drive. Almost every corner featured an apex point that was obscured in some manner from the driver's view at turn in. In some cases that view was disrupted because the corner sloped sharply downhill. In others, the apex was hidden because the track sloped uphill. In others, it was obscured by trees and the radius of the corner itself. Even though none of the corners represented a real racers dilemma, every corner at the track presented a true driving challenge. The track's greatest weakness was that it only had one likely point for out-braking another car- its hairpin.

I always enjoyed racing at Mr. Barber's track.

Book Six: Libera Me

"Deliver me, O Lord, from Eternal Death

On that awful day

When the Heavens and Earth shall be shaken ..."

Chapter Thirty: The Wrecks!

If you race, you will wreck- sooner, or later! You can be as careful as you want, but eventually you will crash- one way or another. Of course, some will certainly crash more than others. But, don't kid yourself that you can avoid "wadding the thing up" every so often. In my almost thirty years of racing I crashed a number of times. This chapter looks back at when that happened.

1. Go Kart- Sebring Club Course:

Shortly after I had completed the Skip Barber school I had an opportunity to race a go kart at Sebring. My neighbor at that time was into karting, and he offered me the use of a kart that belonged to a friend of his. Free racing- who can turn that down?

At the track I discovered that I didn't exactly fit into the tightly fitting, wrap around seat. I was simply a larger dude than the guy who owned the kart. I kind of fit, but then again, not really. I sat more on top of the wrap-around seat, rather than in it. But, what the heck! I wasn't about to let a small thing like not fitting in the seat properly prevent me from going racing.

First corner, first lap, I was forced wide, and then over, the speed bump- like curbing that defined the outside of the turn. As soon as I hit the curbing my lap-belt secured torso flew up, and out of the seat, and then, when the cart slammed down into the pavement, my right-side ribs hammered hard into the rigid edge of the seat. I immediately knew that I'd been hurt, but I didn't let a little thing like that stop me from continuing the race. But, afterwards, as the adrenaline wore off, I realized that I'd fractured a rib, or two. I could hardly move. That was the end of my karting career. I retired from the event and went home. It took a couple of weeks for me to get over that injury.

The moral of this story is never, ever, overlook the element of safety in any racing vehicle.

2. **CRX- Test Day at Hialeah:**

I managed to crash the first race car that I owned- before it ever raced! After CMS had purchased the car from Copper Kettle Racing Mike and I decided that we needed to shake it down before we took it to the first race at Sebring. That's a politically correct way of saying that we couldn't wait to drive the darn thing! Therefore, Mike arranged for us to rent the nearly derelict Hialeah Speedway complex for a day. The road course to be used consisted of a drag strip and parallel return road, which were connected at each end. Not much of a track, but the price was right, and we wanted to drive our new car so badly.

The morning of the test we had rain. But, eventually the track had dried sufficiently to allow us to begin to push fairly hard in the car. Which is what I was doing on what was to have been my last lap on the track- I wanted to set the fastest lap of the test? As I approached the last corner at the end of the back straight I decided to brake deeper than I had done before. I was going for it. But, unfortunately, I locked the front tires, and promptly slid nose first into the tire barrier that lined the outside of the track. It was a sizeable impact. While I wasn't injured, the car came away slightly bent, some bodywork was damaged, and the shock absorber on the left rear was broken. In total, there was probably $2,000 worth of damage. Not a great way to start a brand new racing partnership.

In retrospect, it is clear that when I locked the front tires I should have modulated the brake pedal in order to regain some degree of control. If I would have done that I possibly could have managed to avoid the wall. But, this episode caused me to realize that there was a lot more about driving a race car that I didn't yet know. Therefore, I made the decision to enroll in an upcoming Skip Barber Car Control Clinic course. That was the best money I ever spent! Thank you Terry Earwood.

3. Spec Racer Ford- Gen 2: Sebring Club Course, Cunningham Corner.

Before this weekend I had raced nearly ten years without a crash. In my mind, I had begun to think that crashes were something that usually happened to other people- people who were less careful, and less skilled than me. Silly boy!

This was a typical SCCA Regional Club Race. Mike Scharnow and I were there with our two Spec Racers. Mike's sons, Chris and Geoffry were with him at the track. Sherry and her two sons, Mike and Matt, were with us as well. The race is question was the second of two races for the weekend. For some reason that I can no longer remember Mike had elected to not run the second race. It seems as if he may have had a muscle pull in his neck that made it impossible for him to run the race. And, for some other obscure reason, I thought it would be a good idea if I put the body work from my car (so that the numbers matched) onto his chassis so that I could drive it. I must have thought his car had a stronger engine, or something.

I had qualified towards the back of the Spec Racer field-further back than I thought I should have been. I intended to make up for that in the race. This was a race in which the organizers had combined the Spec Racers together with the Formula V field of cars. These Formula V's were open wheel cars. They had been combined with us because their lap times were just a little slower than ours. Truthfully, they had no business running with our cars. It is never a good idea to combine open wheel cars with closed wheel cars- the potential for calamity is too great. But, that decision had been made by someone else. The Formula V field would start immediately at the rear of the Spec Racer field-no separation between the classes.

At the start I had a very good jump on the cars immediately in front. I knew that with this jump I was going to be able to pass a number of cars. With that goal in mind I worked my way to the inside of the track as the field roared down towards the right angled Cunningham Corner that was the first turn after the start. I delayed my braking for the corner as late as possible, and went to the inside of several Specs that had made more circumspect starts. I had the potential to pass four or five cars by the time we came out of the corner. But, one of the cars that I dove to the inside of was not aware that I was there. As we neared the corner's apex I could feel his car hit the left rear corner of my car. It wasn't enough of an impact to turn me, but it was certainly more than just a tap. But, my immediate sense was that nothing felt damaged. The car seemed fine, so I accelerated out of the corner as usual-my plan seemed to be working as I had intended. The track after Cunningham Corner bends slightly to the left. But, the instant that

I turned the steering wheel in that direction the rear of my car spun violently to the right. At this point there was nothing that I could do but hold on tightly as the car rotated. I understood in that instant that something must have broken in my suspension-probably from the tap the car had just sustained.

As the car spun in the middle of the track the surrounding Spec Racers all made their way safely by. For an instant I thought I was going to escape without serious damage. But, then, the first of the Formula V field arrived on the scene. I believe that they were probably three or four wide, with no place to go. I know for sure that two of them made solid, high speed contact with my car. Several of the other Formula V's ran into the cars that had run into me. By, the time that the spinning stopped, my car had both the front and rear suspensions knocked completely off, and most of the Formula V field was lying scattered around my car. Many of those cars were badly damaged, too. The race was immediately red flagged.

Once everything stopped moving all of the drivers started to take stock of their conditions. I knew that I wasn't injured, and clearly understood that my car was out of the race. So, I climbed out, and started to look at the damage to my vehicle. To my everlasting shame, I noticed that as one of the Formula V drivers exited his car his first concern was not the damage to his car, but whether or not any of his fellow competitors had been injured. I have wished ever since that that had been my first concern, too.

Eventually, all the immobile cars were dragged off the track, and we began to take stock of the damage. My car (actually Mike's car) was clearly going to require an extensive frame and suspension rebuild. It would also need extensive repairs to the fiberglass bodywork. All told- about $6,000 worth of damage. As we looked at the car it quickly became obvious that what had caused the crash was that the initial impact to the left rear had caused the main stud that held the left rear suspension together to shear. Then, as soon as the weight had been transferred off of the left side of the car the bolt had parted and the suspension had come apart.

The only other issue we had to worry about was whether the SCCA would be concerned that the chassis that was damaged was not actually the chassis that I had registered for the race. Fortunately, no one ever noticed that discrepancy.

The primary lesson from all of this mess was that I needed to better balance first lap aggression against good judgment.

4. Spec Racer Ford Gen 2- Sebring Grand Prix Course- Turn 4.

This crash occurred not long after I had transferred the car to Robinson Motor Sports. Along with taking care of the car, Mick had begun to work with me to improve my driving. And, his efforts had worked. In this race I was running in fifth place as the race neared its conclusion- still trying to get into fourth. I was pushing hard, and feeling great about my control over the car. But, with two laps to go a gentle drizzle had begun to fall. Initially, this didn't seem to impact the car's grip at all. I was able to still push hard. On the last lap I was still catching the car in front- I badly wanted to pass him. Turn Three at Sebring is a 90 degree left handed corner. It is immediately followed by a slight bend back to the right that leads into the left hand Carousel Corner. It is critical for a good lap time to carry as much speed as possible into and through the Carousel. I intended to do just that.

But, as I wrestled the car to the right for the high speed bend before the Carousel the rear of the car stepped out to the left, and I spun into the tire wall on the right side of the track. The impact was hard enough to take out the suspension on the left rear of the car. My race was done.

My only conclusion about this crash is that the rain had finally made the track too wet for the speed that I was carrying. I probably should have recognized this and started to take a little more care. In this case, I let my emotions get the best of me- never a good thing in a race car. The price for this miscalculation- a couple thousand dollars worth of damage.

5. Spec Racer Gen 2- Sebring Grand Prix Course- Turn 15.

The occasion was a race at Sebring on the Twelve Hour track. This race coincided with Sherry's 50th birthday. It was a fact of life in our household that we were usually racing on her birthday. But, she wasn't prepared to let this happen when she celebrated her BIG 50! After a great deal of discussion we agreed that we would do this race, but only if she could have all of our kids and grandkids together to help her celebrate this occasion. We, of course, would pick up the hotel and food bills. Sounded like a good deal to me- I got to race! I think Sherry and I were also going to the Bahamas after the race.

So the clan gathered at the track. (As an aside, this is where we first introduced our daughter Anna to our future son-in-law Hector.) I had been working fairly diligently with Mick to improve my driving. As a result, I was now running closer to the front. In this race I had qualified tenth out of a field of over thirty cars. I was close to truly being in the hunt.

As the race started I was all over the back of the cars in front of me. There was no question that I was at least as fast as they were. I could see that the field was being held up by a guy that was obviously driving over his head. He had already slid wide in a couple of corners. I was keeping my eye on him to see what he was going to do next.

I didn't have to wait long. As we approached the right handed Turn 15 he locked up his rear tires, and spun going into the corner. The field of cars was, or course, very tightly packed around him. Most of the cars immediately elected to bail out of the corner by driving off the track to the wide open space on the left. This was obviously the longer way to go, but at least they could avoid the spinning car immediately in front.

Since I was running a few cars further back I had a split second longer to analyze the situation. It seemed to me that there was still room on the inside of the corner to go through safely since the spinning car was in the middle of the track. I made my choice. This route, if it had been successful would have allowed me to come out far in front of all the cars that had bailed off to the left. Third gear, eighty miles per hour- I was committed to the corner.

But, as I reached the apex I could see the spinning car continuing to rotate. And, the driver did not, contrary what you are taught in Skip Barber, have his car's brakes locked. Instead, it was rolling towards the inside of the track- right towards where I was driving. Then, the left front wheel of my car ran over the upward sloping front nose of his car. The momentum of his car, and the forward motion of mine, caused the left side of my car to drive up and over the nose of his car- a nose that now was effectively a launching ramp. My car flew high in the air, while slowing rolling to the right. It eventually came down, thirty yards or so later, squarely on top of its roll bar. The car then rebounded, and rolled completely over one more time- just for good measure. It finally stopped bouncing with the car's wheels in the air, and with the roll bar keeping the car's weight off of the driver. For my part, I was still securely strapped in place, hanging upside down.

As I hung there, silently contemplating what had just happened, my initial concern was fire. No one wants to be trapped in a burning car. Fortunately, I couldn't smell, or see, any sign of smoke or leaking gasoline. I reached behind me and turned off the car's electrical master switch, and began to contemplate how best to exit the car. As I hung there I noticed that one of the competitors, Larry Baisden, drove up alongside to see if I required assistance. I was able to give him a thumbs up sign (it might have actually been a thumbs down sign!) Satisfied that I was OK, he then drove off to reenter the race. I very much appreciated this show of concern on his part. I then propped myself off the ground with one arm, and released my belts with the other. Much to my relief I slid gently onto the pavement, and began to squirm out from under the car. By the time I extricated myself a couple of corner workers appeared, and led me over to the inside concrete wall, where they suggested that I have a seat. Shortly after that an ambulance drove up. The medics took charge, and eventually had me enter the back of the vehicle. While they took my vitals they enquired about whether I was OK. I told them, "Yeah, I am now. But, I won't be after my wife see's what I did to the car!" We all laughed. Eventually, they concluded that I was no worse for wear. Surprisingly, the car was also relatively undamaged. The crash crew was actually able to tow it back to the pits- with me in it steering. The car did need work before it would be able to race again- bodywork, roll cage repair, a few suspension pieces, and a new radiator. Nothing that another $6,000 wouldn't fix.

What made this wreck even worse was that I knew that I could have actually been able to avoid it if I would have bailed to the left. I had gotten greedy, and it had cost me. Jeeeeez. Another expensive weekend. I think subconsciously after that I stopped worrying so much about getting faster and closer to the front of the field. I guess, maybe, I finally started to grow up.

6. Spec Racer Ford- Gen 2- Sebring Grand Prix Course- Turn 17.

A large field of cars on the long course at Sebring. On the first lap, in Turn 3, there was a stack up of cars as everyone fought for the advantageous inner line. I remember that someone hit my car in the rear, but I didn't sense that any damage had been done. I looked in the mirrors but couldn't see anything out of the ordinary. I set about trying to aggressively race towards the front.

As we sped down the back straight towards Turn 17 it seemed as if the car was making good speed. I was closing on the group of cars in front. There was a car close behind, but he didn't seem to have a run. My sense was that there was no way that he was going to be able to make a pass. I drove to my customary turn-in point (at the 225 yard mark) and then steered to the right, aiming just to the left of the tip of the concrete wall that protruded from the inside. I was still at full speed, pedal flat to the floor, moving at roughly 135 miles per hour. But, the instant that I turned the wheel, the rear of the car stepped out, and rotated to the left. For an instant I was heading, head first, at the upcoming solid concrete wall, at full speed. I knew that this was not going to be pretty- I was in big trouble!

I slammed on the brakes. That allowed the car to continue to rotate around. A second later the left rear of the car impacted the wall- hard. The shock was instantaneous and hard. Then, the car continued to rotate around and the right front of the car slammed the wall. Fortunately, I had remembered to let go of the steering wheel before the front of the car made impact. As it turned out, the car had impacted the wall at an angle- it was a glancing blow, rather than a head on stop that can kill a driver. From that point the car spun on across the track. It finally came to a stop more than a hundred yards from where it had first made contact. It was well off the racing surface. In fact, it was so far out of the way that the race was eventually able to be restarted without the workers even having to move the car further!

As soon as the car stopped I began to assess my condition. I remember being somewhat surprised that nothing seemed to hurt. I then slowly began to un-strap my belts, and to think about climbing out of the car. When I finally got out of the car- I was completely at a loss about what had just happened. There should have been no way that the car would have spun where it did- there was not enough centrifugal force there to cause that. I could see that the car was damaged, but it looked like all the suspension was still attached, and the tires were inflated. That was not the reason for the spin. But, for the life of me, something about the car looked amiss. Then it dawned on me, the rear bodywork of the car was missing. I looked around, expecting to see remnants of fiberglass littering the track. But, there was nothing. When the corner workers reached me I asked them whether they knew what had happened to the tail of the car. They looked at me like I was crazy. The tail was simply missing.

At that point I began to develop a theory about what might have happened. I assumed that the tail could have come off the car when it had been hit from the rear- early in the lap. Then, I assumed that the car's normal level of down force was absent when I turned at top speed into Turn 17. For the life of me that was the only explanation for what had just happened. When the race ended the workers used a wrecker to pick up me and the car and took us to the RMS trailer. Eventually, I told Mick what I thought had happened. He confirmed that the tail had come off the car, but indicated that he didn't think that this would have caused a reduction in down force. But, for the life of me, I didn't know what else to think. And, truthfully, I was still somewhat in a mild state of shock. Hitting a solid wall at over 130 miles per hour will do that to you.

An hour or so later, as Sherry and I drove back to Pine Island, I called Mick again. I needed to pick his brain about what might have happened. I was still spooked. That was when he told me that another driver had stopped by his trailer after we had left to apologize for having hit me going into Turn 17. As it turned out the nose of his car had slightly contacted my right rear wheel when I turned into the corner. He told Mick that he thought I had gone too deep into the corner. To me that would not explain why he was where he was at that moment. But, for whatever reason, he was surprised when I turned in when I did. Mick said that there were smudges of yellow paint from that driver's car on my tire. It had been such a slight tap that I hadn't even felt it. But, it had been enough to spin my car. But, at least, I was relieved to finally understand what had caused the crash. In my mind I had been spun out, certainly not intentionally, but spun out, none the less. A racing incident as they say- just a slight misjudgment on someone's part.

As it transpired, for two years after this crash, my neck would periodically hurt. My regular doctor even transferred me to a specialist to have it examined. The specialist x-rayed it, but couldn't find anything. But, I'm still convinced that this pain was related to the instantaneous shock I felt when my car hit that wall at 130 miles per hour. Eventually, thankfully, the neck pain has largely disappeared.

Was this crash my fault? I don't think so. Granted, I didn't see the guy to the inside- because at the moment he moved to the inside my eyes were focused on the cars, and the corner, ahead. Still, the guy who hit me should not have been where he was. But, "that's racing," as they say! I was very lucky that I wasn't seriously injured in this crash.

I was also lucky that I wasn't seriously injured in nearly thirty years of racing. Very lucky! During this period several folks that I raced with had almost lost their lives driving the same type of car, in the same type of races. Luck certainly plays a role. Anyone who straps themselves into a race car needs to understand that they too can be hurt, or even killed.

In looking back at all of these crashes almost all of them are ultimately attributable to "driver error"- usually mine! There's no question that a driver needs to be careful- at the same time that they are driving their fool heads off, trying to go as fast as possible, being as aggressive as they know how. The constant balance between these opposites is what makes racing so difficult, and so attractive.

Book Seven: Benedictus

"Blessed is he that cometh in the name of the Lord...."

Chapter Thirty One: Twelve Speed Secrets

Many, many books have been written about how to drive a race car. I know, because I've read most of them. And, despite all of that knowledge, I still was never particularly quick- leading me to respect the words of some forgotten NASCAR crew chief- "It's a lot easier to slow them down, than it is to speed them up!" I'm a firm believer the really quick drivers are usually blessed with an innate ability that others simply don't possess. But, that isn't to say that things can't be done to help most drivers drive more quickly. In this chapter, I want to share some of the things that helped me over the years.

1. **Fundamentals:** You will never consistently go fast if you don't know the basic techniques of racing. By that I'm primarily referring to driving the proper racing line: Turn-in; Apex; Track-out. One of the greatest lessons I ever received in a racing car was having the opportunity in one Firehawk race to follow Terry Earwood for a short while after he had lapped me. What I observed was that Terry, Skip Barber's Chief Instructor, really practiced what he preached- he didn't leave any distance between his tires and the edge of the road- not at turn in, apex, or track out. His driving was extremely precise! My car placement, on the other hand, was sloppier. I commonly left a foot, or so, of unused track at all of these key points. The consequence was that my racing line was shorter, and slower, than Terry's. If we were both driving at the limit of adhesion, I simply couldn't carry as much speed through the corner as he was able to.

2. **Use a Late Apex:** Lance Stewart, a great champion, always preaches the benefits of using, when possible, a late corner apex. Not only does this approach create the opportunity to get power down earlier and longer, but it also helps to provide a safety cushion on exit. Remember, "he who gets the power down first- wins."

3. **Footwork:** To be successful in racing you can't make errors. Being precise in your footwork is one of the very best way to limit errors.

4. **Braking:** Using a proper braking technique is, paradoxically, critical to going quickly. One of the sayings in racing is "Brakes are like lawyers- they cost you every time you use them." But, unfortunately, in racing you do have to use your brakes- and often. What's important is that you use them correctly. When you first apply the brakes you want to apply hard, firm pressure against the pedal- of course, you don't really want to slam on the brakes, but when you brake- you do want to brake very hard. If displayed graphically, the initial pressure on the pedal should show a nearly vertical, upward sloping line. You don't want to ease on the pedal in an effort to be smooth. Instead, you want to use all of the brakes capacity to slow the car as soon as possible. As you do, the resulting deceleration will cause a transfer of weight onto the front wheels- allowing them to use the full force of braking to slow the car. The graph should then, for a short period, show a nearly stable plateau of steady pressure. But, once your speed begins to slow, that transferred weight will gradually rebound towards the rear. As that occurs, you will need to ease pressure off of the brake pedal. The pressure graph will then begin to trail downward. The goal is to brake as hard as you can at all

times without locking up the tires. In other words, you want to maintain the tires on the threshold of lockup, i.e., "threshold braking." As you steer in towards the apex you will still want to keep a gradually decreasing pressure on the pedal. This, in a nut shell, is the concept of trail braking- you want to gradually trail pressure off of the brake pedal as the car's speed slows and as you turn in towards the apex. Using this approach will help you to brake marginally deeper, and to turn the car without losing time. As you consider this concept it is important to remember that a tire can only do so much work. You can use all of that capacity for braking; or use it all for cornering; or you can use it for some combination of both, e.g. 60% for braking, 40% for cornering. But, if you should exceed that 100% threshold, the tire will then stop gripping the track, and instead, begin to slide. A driver who is trail braking is continually adjusting, in real time, the % of the tire's work that is being used for braking, versus handling. For most people, trail braking works best in slower corners. Most people don't want, or need, to trail brake into fast corners- in them you've got more important things to worry about.

Another important point to learn about braking is how to determine the point at which to apply the brakes. Bottom line- you need to discover this point incrementally. You'll need to start by braking at a point that is clearly too early. Then, the next lap, you incrementally move that point further in before you brake. If you are still too early, then you go a bit further the next lap. Critically, you want to do this in relatively small increments. You never want to take a huge leap at finding the proper braking spot. Such a leap may put you well beyond the appropriate braking point, and into the wall. So, just keep moving the braking point in until you reach the distance where, when you turn in, your speed is too great to be able to apex at the proper point. Then, back it up a foot, or two, and try again. Soon you know exactly where your braking point is. Of course, as the track cools or heats, or as fluid is spilled, or as the track gets dirty over the course of a race weekend, this point may change slightly. So, you always have to pay attention to ensuring that you are braking at the point that is as deep into the corner as you can go. But, once you know that point, don't keep trying to go deeper. You'll just create mistakes for yourself. And, once you know where that point is, use it to your advantage when battling against other cars. If a competitor in a similar car tries to pass you by braking deeper, you should understand that they are not going to be able to do so- they will simply slide wide past the point where they need to turn in. Be prepared for this to happen, and when it does simply turn underneath that car as it slides towards the outside of the track.

Another point to talk about with respect to braking is adjusting brake pedal bias (i.e., the percentage of braking being done by the front versus the rear wheels). In general, in dry weather you will want to be able to lock up your front tires before your rears do. But, you don't want to dial so much pressure out of the rears that they can't do any work. You want the rears to work as hard as they can, but just up to the point of lock-up. As you approach that point, you can feel the rear of the car begin to feel squirrely under braking. When that happens, dial in a little more front brake, and you'll be good to go. The brake pedal pressure adjustment is an important control. In the wet, since you will have to apply the brakes more gently, the amount of weight transferred to the front tires will be reduced. Therefore, you will probably need to dial in relatively more rear wheel brake bias.

The final point about braking is making sure that you are not over slowing the car. In my experience that was the hardest thing for me to do. Commonly, I would slow the car too much before turning to the apex, and beginning to applying power. Mentally, I guess I needed to make sure that I was always in control. This approach did allow me to stay generally out of trouble. But, losing a tenth of a second in each corner soon adds up, over all the turns on a track, to the loss of real time. Eventually, I learned that I needed to actively guard against doing this, and to focus instead on carrying enough speed into and through the middle part of the corner so that either the front or rear of my car was constantly only the verge of sliding. Of course, you don't want to actually cause the car to slide, but you want to be as close to that as possible.

5. **Acceleration:**

In general, you can crush the brake pedal; but, you need to treat the accelerator more gently. Some even say to treat the accelerator as if there is the proverbial raw egg between your foot and the pedal. A driver certainly has to treat the accelerator with respect- feeding in only as much power as the tires can handle as they struggle to accomplish the multiple demands a driver is making of them (remember 100%). But, this is not at all the same thing as being lazy with going to the accelerator. You cannot afford to waste even the smallest fraction of a second in going to power. You have to be alert at all times about what is happening as you feed in the power- because you want to get to full power as soon as possible. He who goes to power first (and holds it) usually wins the race.

6. The Start of the Race:

"The easiest time to pass someone is at the start!"

"Races are seldom won at the start; but, they are frequently lost there!"

In my opinion, these two seemingly conflicting statements are both equally true. Drivers do need to be **very** aggressive at the start. But, they also always need to be careful, alert, and thoughtful.

I have a number of suggestions regarding starts.

a. Stay extremely close behind the car in front- don't give away any more time than necessary by lagging back. Stay tight.

b. Try to anticipate the flag falling. Your ability to pass the car in front is going to depend upon whether you can go to power before he does- we're talking about fractions of a second. And, then, once you go to power, you must stay at full power, trying to **never lift**, until it is time to brake for the next corner. Many drivers tend to be overly cautious at the start. This caution sometimes allows a driver at full power to simply drive past the more cautious driver as you approach the first corner.

c. If you are lucky enough to be starting on the pole, remember that you control the start. You get to decide, within whatever limits have been set by the race officials, when to go to power. You need to use this advantage to try to surprise the driver alongside you by going to power first. And, in this regard, it is important to remember that the flagman, since he is usually looking at you head on, is going to have a difficult time determining exactly when you go to power. Therefore, you do have an opportunity, within limits, to go to full power early. And, doing this can help to ensure that you have a clear run into the first corner.

d. Before the start, think about where you will most easily be able to pass. It may be on the inside of the track. The Club Course at Sebring, where the first three "real corners" after the start are tight right-handers, is a great example of where the inside of the track is preferred. At Daytona, on the other hand, the outside line into Turn One is frequently left wide open as cars tend to bunch up on the inside. And, being on this side of the track may give you an advantaged position as you approach the right handed carousel corner that follows. Of course, you do always need to be flexible at the start- there is no way of predicting what will actually happen- you need to be able to take advantage of whatever opportunities present themselves.

e. Having said all the above- don't be "**That Guy!**" Don't do stupid stuff at the start that screws up everybody's race. Be aggressive, but always be smart, and be careful. Cars at the start are closer together than they will ever be again during a race. This presents the opportunity for both rewards, and risk. Always be aware, and alert. And, try to not put anyone, or their equipment, at risk.

7. The Most Important Corners:

In general, the most important corners on any track will be "the fastest corners that lead on to the longest straights." Of course, every corner is important, but you should focus especially on doing well those fast corners that lead onto long straights. You need to carry as much speed through those corners as you can, so that you can carry that extra speed all the way down the following straight. At Sebring I always focused on Turns 1, 16, and 17. At Daytona, I wanted to make sure I got "The Bus Stop", and Turn 6 done properly. At Palm Beach you need to carry as much speed as you can onto the long back straight.

8. **Passing:**

One of the most important skills in racing is be able to pass another car. The best way to do that is, of course, to be able to drive by them going down the straight. To do that you've got to go through the preceding corner faster; and, then use the draft created by the car you are overtaking to the fullest extent possible- remember, a draft is essentially "free horsepower." If you can go through the corner faster, and if you draft, you'll more likely than not be able to pull out and pass the car ahead. Of course, you'll want to pull out on the side that gives you the inside line going into the next corner. Then, just go to your normal braking point, and assuming you are ahead of, or still alongside, the car being passed, you own the corner. Take your normal line, and the car being passed will usually have to give way.

But, make sure you are fully alongside the car being overtaken before you attempt a pass. If your head isn't at least even with the head of the driver that you are overtaking then you should probably back out of the corner. If you can't see him, he probably can't see you either. Of course, this is not to say that you shouldn't try to work the driver you are attempting to pass by showing a feint to the inside. Sometimes that driver, particularly if they are inexperienced, will give the corner to you by braking early. But, don't try to force the issue if you aren't clearly alongside the car you are trying to pass. Any experienced driver will simply close the door on you, leaving you the options of backing out, or crashing. Again, don't be "That Guy" who tries to dive inside to make a pass when they don't really have the corner. It is probably not going to work out well. And, after the race you are probably just going to end up in a silly argument about who was at fault. If you are not fully alongside, don't try to pass.

9. **Mistakes:**

Just do the math. Mistakes cost you a lot of time on the track. If you try to go too fast, and end up spinning the car, you can easily lose twenty seconds, or more, to the cars around you as you regain control, and then try to safely re-enter the track. Your lap times will have to be a heck of a lot faster than the lap times of those around you to ever make-up that amount of time. Winners don't make mistakes- big, or small. If you look at the lap times of those at the top of the field they are usually very consistent- varying from lap to lap only by a tenth or two. But, as you go through the field you will notice that lap times for those farther back usually show more variability. Those drivers further back may even have the fastest overall lap times, but they will also have laps where their times are, for some reason, off the pace. This inconsistency is generally the result of making mistakes- trying to brake too deeply; trying to take a corner too quickly, trying to make an ill advised pass. The time you lose from mistakes is always difficult to recover.

10. **Keep Your Eyes Up!**

The eyes of the driver are his most important resource. It is critical that the driver keeps his eyes up, looking far down the track, and critically, looking, not at what is immediately in front, but rather at where he wants the car to go next. Your brain is an amazing computer- it doesn't have to be consciously thinking about what to do immediately if it is already looking out into the future. Drivers that keep their eyes up, and look ahead, will notice that the speed at which things occur in front of them slows dramatically- giving you more time to react. Remember, the brain is able to compute subconsciously. You don't actually have to look directly at what is immediately in front of the car in order for the brain to be aware of it, and adjust accordingly! Keep your eyes up, and looking at where you want to go **next**.

11. **Just Drive the Damn Thing:**

At the end of the day, to be fast, you've got to drive the thing- hard! And, the only way to be able to do that safely, and consistently, is to do all the little things correctly, while still pushing to the limits of adhesion the four little screaming patches of rubber that connect the car to the track. Remember what Terry Earwood has always said- "A squealing tire is a happy tire!" You can do everything correctly, but if you are not pushing hard, you are not going to go fast. I know- because I've done that. If possible, try to develop the ability to feel, and to understand simultaneously, what is happening at each of those four separate rubber patches.

12. **Don't Lollygag Under Yellow:**

This is not really a speed secret- it's a pet peeve! When a full course yellow is thrown the stewards want you to close up into a tight pack as quickly as safely possible. Of course, they want you to use all necessary care when negotiating the scene of an accident where workers and others may be at risk. But, they do not want you to then simply drive slowly around the rest of the track. You need to drive as quickly as you safely can to close up to the pack in front. This is important because the stewards won't feel that they can safely release the wreckers, ambulances, and workers to deal with the accident until the cars are under the control of the pace car. Additionally, a full course yellow is your opportunity to close up o the cars in front of you- to make up the ground that you've lost in the course of the race. Don't waste this opportunity!

Most people, even after reading these words of wisdom, are not going to be able to sit in a car for the first time, and immediately be fast. To go fast, you are going to need a lot of "Seat Time." In other words, you are going to need to practice, practice, and practice so that at a sub-conscious level you can anticipate what a car is going to do before it even does it, and understand, without even thinking about it, what you need to do to control the car when it does that. The ability to do this only comes from getting "seat time." The more time you can spend driving a race car, ultimately, the better you are going to be. Of course, most of us can't afford to drive real race cars that often. But, any kind of driving at the limit can be helpful. Most pros start by driving "go-karts." Club Racing- especially, Endurance Racing, is another great way to get a lot of seat time. Autocrossing, and rallying are other excellent ways to develop car feel and control. You don't have to go fast to learn.

And, it always helps to spend time observing what the faster drivers on the track do to go fast. In my experience, while they may have some things that they do differently from each other, what they have in common is that they all do the basics- well. They hit their marks, they are precise, they know how to brake and accelerate, and they don't make mistakes. Don't get sucked into believing that somehow they are braver, or have bigger balls, or any of that nonsense. They simply know how, and have the ability, to drive race cars well. And, most of them have developed that skill over a long period of time. And, with that they have developed a fine sense of car control. Those are the things it takes to go quickly in a race car.

In Paradisum

(In a Requiem, the chant or refrain traditionally sung by the choir as the body is taken out of the church. Interestingly, this piece served as the inspiration for "When the Saints Go Marching In.")

"May the angels lead you into paradise

May the martyrs receive you at your arrival

And lead you into the holy city of Jerusalem

May choirs of angels receive you

May you have eternal rest."

Chapter Thirty Two: In Conclusion

"You'll probably love racing- if the idea of driving around in circles, throwing away hundred dollar bills, sounds like a good idea!"

The above quote is one I've often used, humorously and self-deprecatingly, to try to explain racing to folks outside of the sport. Because, at the end of the day, in a nut shell, and at a very fundamental level, this is what it comes down to. Most of us are simply driving repeatedly around a track, and paying a fair amount of money to do it. And, when looked at in this way, it is difficult to realistically argue that this sport is one that any intelligent person would wish to pursue.

But, of course, there is more to it than that. I hope that the preceding chapters have gone someway to help explain the attraction, the appeal, and even the addiction, that many of us have to the sport. An activity that is one of the most difficult things to do well that most humans will ever attempt. That is part of the sport's attraction- driving a racing car quickly is a very hard thing to do well. It is also a very dangerous thing to do. In my years of racing, while I was only seriously injured once- driving a go kart- I personally knew many people who were seriously injured, and, in a few cases, even killed. Willingly putting your body, and even your life, on the line is an intrinsic part of the sport's allure. As Hemingway reportedly once said: "There are only three sports: mountain climbing, bull fighting, and auto racing. The rest are merely games."

Does this make racing an intelligent thing to do? Of course, it doesn't. But, it always seemed to me that the very real risk that you encounter ever time you buckle yourself into a race car does, in some way, tend to lend an essential, and fundamental, sanctity to the activity. Every time that I approached a corner like Road America's "Kink" I was intentionally, and consciously, balancing my very life against the challenge of doing something- that was difficult- well. Somehow, that always meant something to me.

And, every time that I put my foot to the floor at the start of a race, roaring towards a distant first turn, literally inches away from dozens of other similarly focused speeding men and machines I somehow entered a different realm- a realm where life's daily common sense, and restraints, were temporarily suspended- otherwise, how else could anyone ever do this? We all understood that the slightest miscalculation, or poorly judged move, on anyone's part, could instantly turn the whole field of beautiful, expensive racing machines into nothing more than a big smoldering, steaming pile of junk. We'd all seen it happen before. But, being willing to overlook that potential outcome- to me- always, somehow, meant something.

And, what about the pure joy of successfully sliding a car, at over a hundred miles per hour through a corner with the vehicle securely balanced on the absolute limit of control? Surely, the mere accomplishment of that dangerous ballet has to mean something!

But, of course, we all know that, at the end of the day, it probably won't mean much to anybody. Perhaps, if we are lucky, there may be a forgotten entry of results buried deeply in a dusty record book somewhere. Or, maybe, there will be a stock of inexpensive plastic trophies- trinkets that will eventually be condemned to a trash dump as soon as the only person to whom they meant anything has been ushered off the stage.

In all likelihood, Shakespeare's Hamlet had it right after all when he depressingly muttered to himself:

"Tomorrow, and tomorrow, and tomorrow

Creeps in this petty pace from day to day,

To the last syllable of recorded time;

And all our yesterdays have lighted fools

The way to dusty death. Out, out, brief candle!

Life's but a walking shadow, a poor player

That struts and frets his hour upon the stage

And then is heard no more. It is a tale

Told by an idiot, full of sound and fury,

Signifying nothing.

- Macbeth (Act 5, lines 17-28)

It is very easy, of course, for one to say that racing **is** essentially nothing- just an idiotic activity. And, without doubt, it is certainly full of sound and fury. But, I can only hope that, somehow, having done a thing so difficult, so dangerous, and so beautiful, for so long may, in some obscure way, have helped to enliven, and decorate, what otherwise would have been a relatively undistinguished progression from cradle to grave.

I know for certain that I had fun doing it! But, saying that I did all of this simply to have fun somehow diminishes it. It's hard to believe that any reasonable person would devote such a large portion of their lives to doing something so difficult, so dangerous, so selfish, so time consuming, and so expensive just for fun. Without question there were many times when we were definitely not having much fun. Tiredly, and sleepily,

292

driving the rig back home to Florida after the 24-hour race in Watkins Glen, New York stands out as one of those less than fun times. Packing up, and paying for, wrecked race cars was never much fun, either. Truthfully, there were a whole lot of times that we had to do things that were not exactly fun. But, still we raced.

In my mind, truthfully, I never raced just to have fun. To some extent, in some basic way, I may have raced simply because I had to- it was just a part of who I was. But, I don't think that's the total explanation, either. There can be no doubt that I always made the decision to race-deliberately. Without question, without doubt, I always raced because I wanted to. And, I think I may have wanted to race so much because of the strongest of all emotions- love. I raced not just because I loved doing it- although I certainly did that. But, rather, at a more fundamental level, I raced because of my love for the sport.

Thanks to all who helped me do this. I love you all.

Made in the USA
Columbia, SC
05 February 2023

11703035R00161